MORE CREATIVE COPING SKILLS
FOR CHILDREN

by the same author

Creative Coping Skills for Children
Emotional Support through Arts and Crafts Activities
ISBN 978 1 84310 921 1
eISBN 978 1 84642 954 5

Creative Expression Activities for Teens
Exploring Identity through Art, Craft and Journaling
ISBN 978 1 84905 842 1
eISBN 978 0 85700 417 8

How to Get Kids Offline, Outdoors, and Connecting with Nature
200+ Creative Activities to Encourage Self-esteem, Mindfulness, and Wellbeing
ISBN 978 1 84905 968 8
eISBN 978 0 85700 853 4

of related interest

The Big Book of Therapeutic Activity Ideas for Children and Teens
Inspiring Arts-Based Activities and Character Education Curricula
Lindsey Joiner
ISBN 978 1 84905 865 0
eISBN 978 0 85700 447 5

The Big Book of EVEN MORE Therapeutic Activity Ideas for Children and Teens
Inspiring Arts-Based Activities and Character Education Curricula
Lindsey Joiner
ISBN 978 1 84905 749 3
eISBN 978 1 78450 196 9

Creating Children's Art Games for Emotional Support
Vicky Barber
ISBN 978 1 84905 163 7
eISBN 978 0 85700 409 3

Focusing and Calming Games for Children
Mindfulness Strategies and Activities to Help Children to Relax, Concentrate and Take Control
Deborah M. Plummer
Illustrated by Jane Serrurier
ISBN 978 1 84905 143 9
eISBN 978 0 85700 344 7

MORE CREATIVE COPING SKILLS FOR CHILDREN

ACTIVITIES, GAMES, STORIES, AND HANDOUTS TO HELP CHILDREN SELF REGULATE

Bonnie Thomas

Jessica Kingsley *Publishers*
London and Philadelphia

First published in 2016
by Jessica Kingsley Publishers
73 Collier Street
London N1 9BE, UK
and
400 Market Street, Suite 400
Philadelphia, PA 19106, USA

www.jkp.com

Library of Congress Cataloging in Publication Data
Names: Thomas, Bonnie, 1971- author.
Title: More creative coping skills for children : activities, games, stories
    and handouts to help children self-regulate / Bonnie Thomas.
Description: Philadelphia : Jessica Kingsley Publishers, 2016.
Identifiers: LCCN 2016002154 | ISBN 9781785920219 (alk. paper)
Subjects: LCSH: Children--Life skills guides. | Child development. | Emotions
    in children. | Self-control in children. | Creative activities and seat
    work.
Classification: LCC HQ767.9 .T486 2016 | DDC 305.231--dc23 LC
record available at https://lccn.loc.gov/2016002154

British Library Cataloguing in Publication Data
A CIP catalogue record for this book is available from the British Library

ISBN 978 1 78592 021 9
eISBN 978 1 78450 267 6

Printed and bound in the United States

Contents

Chapter 12 Traumatic Events and Illnesses **205**

Chapter 13 Family Challenges **221**

Introduction

. . . .

More Creative Coping Skills for Children is a comprehensive resource for professionals who work with children. It is also a resource for parents and guardians. The book provides interventions that encourage children to learn and use coping strategies regarding relationships, emotions, behaviors, and life experiences. Each chapter highlights a group of mild to moderately challenging behaviors that children might experience, and that commonly occur together. For example, one chapter will focus on basic manners and interpersonal skills. Another chapter will focus on paying attention and listening. Throughout the book you will find activities, stories, affirmations, and parent/child handouts to help you address particular behaviors and challenges, as well as the following features:

! Challenges

This defines the situation, feeling, or behavior that the child is struggling with.

◎ Goals

This section provides one or more goals that a child might be working toward. The goals are written primarily for counselors who write treatment plans with their clients, but they also provide parents with a framework for defining goals.

Skills

The activities and interventions provided in each chapter promote skill building specific to the challenges noted. For example, Chapter 4 on Anger Management has activities and interventions that build on skills such as recognizing triggers and diffusing anger safely and respectfully.

 ## Interventions

Interventions in the book include creative play, arts and crafts activities, games, coloring pages, and/or worksheets. All of the activities in this book encourage skill-building related to the behaviors and challenges featured in each chapter.

Handouts contain lists of interventions to try and/or other helpful pieces of information pertaining to a chapter. If you are a professional who works with children and families, the handouts provide something concrete that clients can take home for their own use.

 ## An accompanying story

The stories in each chapter focus on a character's behavior or challenge that the child might also be struggling with. The stories provide a means for children to learn about their own behaviors or experiences in a child-friendly manner, via storytelling. Stories are a gentle way to approach issues with children because it is easier for some children to talk about a character in a story rather than themselves.

 ## An activity to go along with the story

I have included an activity to go along with each story. The activities reinforce some of the skills noted in the story and/or provide a quick and easy craft to engage the child in further discussion about the story.

 ## Affirmations

Affirmations are brief empowering statements that a child can use for "self-talk," mantras, or reminders (e.g. "I can do this"). When used consistently, affirmations can help to increase positive thinking and confidence.

CHAPTER 1

Building Interpersonal and Social Skills

 ## Challenges

The child has difficulty making and keeping friends.

The child struggles with general social skills.

Goals

The child will gain new skills in making and keeping friends.

The child will sustain a friendship for more than a month.

Skill: Using basic manners

Manners are important for children to practice and use because manners are a way to show respect to others. When children do not use their manners it can negatively impact their relationships. Role model the manners you want the child to use and praise the child when they use them. Praise will reinforce the child's desire to continue using good manners.

Interventions

Tea parties are a wonderful way to practice manners. Have pretend tea parties with children to practice the basics in saying please and thank you, using table manners, and showing kind regard to others. As the child masters the use of manners, move on to the reward of having "real" tea parties with actual tea and treats.

CAPTAIN'S QUARTERS GAME

Captain's Quarters is a game where players become pirates at a meal where they must use their best manners. The game has silly scenarios that make talking about manners fun. The game board features pirates sitting at the Captain's table with empty dinner plates in front of them. Players take turns answering the cards (youngest player goes first). Each time a player answers a card correctly, the player puts a coin or bottle cap on one of the empty dinner plates. Fill all of the dinner plates at the table to finish the game. This is a cooperative game, so everybody wins when all of the plates are full.

Number of players: 1

Object of the game: To get through dinner using your best manners

Materials

- Captain's Quarters Game sheet

- Pirate Cards

- Various coins or bottle caps

Directions

Your game board features pirates sitting at the Captain's table with empty dinner plates in front of them. Each time you answer one of the cards, put a coin or bottle cap on the dinner plate. Fill all of the dinner plates to finish the game.

Pirate Cards

Bramblebeard accidentally lets out a loud burp at the table. What should he say afterwards?

1. "Oh my! That was a loud one!"

2. "Argh!!!!! Now that's the sound of a well-fed pirate!"

3. "Excuse me. Pardon me. My apologies."

Cabinlass Jilly would like some buttered biscuits, but they are way down at the other end of the table. What's the most polite way she can ask for them?

1. "For the love of gravy, get those biscuits down at my end of the table!"

2. "Blackbeard, would you be so kind as to pass the biscuits this way, please?"

3. Toss a goblet at the person closest to the biscuits to get their attention and then yell, "I want some biscuits!"

Pricklebeard Pete is drinking too much rum at the table and he is starting to get loud and rude. What is something you and the other pirates could do to keep this situation from getting out of control?

Silverblade Samuel has arrived and he is looking for a place to sit at the table. Should you:

1. Scoot over and make room for him?

2. Ignore him and hope someone else makes room for him?

3. Tell him there is no room at the table for any more guests.

Ravenheart loves roasted carrots. There is a small bowl of roasted carrots for everybody to share. How do you think the other pirates will respond if Ravenheart takes more than his share of the carrots?

Grim O'Malley starts to tell jokes and stories at the table that are not appropriate for company. What should you or the other pirates do?

Salty Bones starts to tease One Tooth Eddie about having only one tooth. What do you think One Tooth Eddie and/or the other pirates should do?

Darkbeard has a gazillion biscuit crumbs stuck in his beard. Do you

1. Try to get his attention and discreetly let him know?

2. Laugh at him?

3. Fill your own beard with crumbs and say, "Look at me! I'm Darkbeard!"

Rapscallion Red has a terrible cold. What should he do if he needs to cough or sneeze?

1. Sneeze and cough into his sleeve.

2. Sneeze and cough into the sleeve of the pirate sitting next to him.

3. Sneeze and cough all over the dinner table.

One Tooth Eddie wants to know whether it's polite to talk with food in your mouth.

Davey Dreggs needs to use the bathroom during dinner. When he gets to the bathroom, the door is closed. Should Davey

1. Walk right in?

2. Knock on the door and then only go into the bathroom if no one answers?

3. Yell: "Hey—if someone is in there, hurry up!!!!"

On your way to the dinner table you accidentally bump into Scallywag Scott. Do you say

1. "Hey! Get out of my way!"

2. "Excuse me—sorry I bumped into you!"

3. "Argh, Matey! I wouldn't bump into you if you weren't in my way!"

Barnacle Bob opens the cabin door for other pirates when they come into the cabin. Is this a polite thing to do?

*

Plunderin' Paul keeps interrupting the pirate Captain and the Queen's guest. How do you think this makes them feel?

Grubby Sparrow keeps getting distracted by his pet parrot, which is sitting on his shoulder. What should Grubby Sparrow do to focus better on the conversation at the table?

Cabinlass Kate wants to know if she has to be on time for dinner. What would you tell her?

Black Knuckle needs a knife to cut his food. He doesn't see one next to his plate but the pirate sitting next to him has one. Should Black Knuckle

1. Grab the knife and use it?

2. Complain loudly that there is no knife next to his plate?

3. Ask the pirate: "Could I use your knife for a moment, please?"

Curlybeard Curt was up all night washing the ship deck. Is it okay for him to sleep during the rest of the meal once he has eaten?

Scurvy Dawg Douglas is all done with his meal and he has left his dirty plate, napkin, and utensils on the table for someone else to clean up. Is this a polite thing to do?

Farley Fibs-a-Lot is wondering whether he is supposed to thank the Captain for inviting him to dinner. What do you think?

Buccaneer Ben needs to tell Swashbuckler Sasha something. What's a polite way to get her attention?

1. Kick her under the table.

2. Throw a biscuit at her.

3. Say: "Excuse me, Sasha, I need to tell you something."

Dinner is on the Captain's table and almost everyone is seated. When can Maddie the Map Ripper start eating?

1. Right away.

2. When everyone is seated and the Captain indicates it's time to eat.

Planky McSplinters has gravy in his moustache. What should he do?

1. Use his sleeve to wipe the gravy off.

2. Try to lick and slurp the gravy off.

3. Use a napkin to wipe the gravy away.

Bowman Bailey is wondering whether he should thank or compliment the cook after the meal. What do you think?

CAPTAIN'S QUARTERS GAME

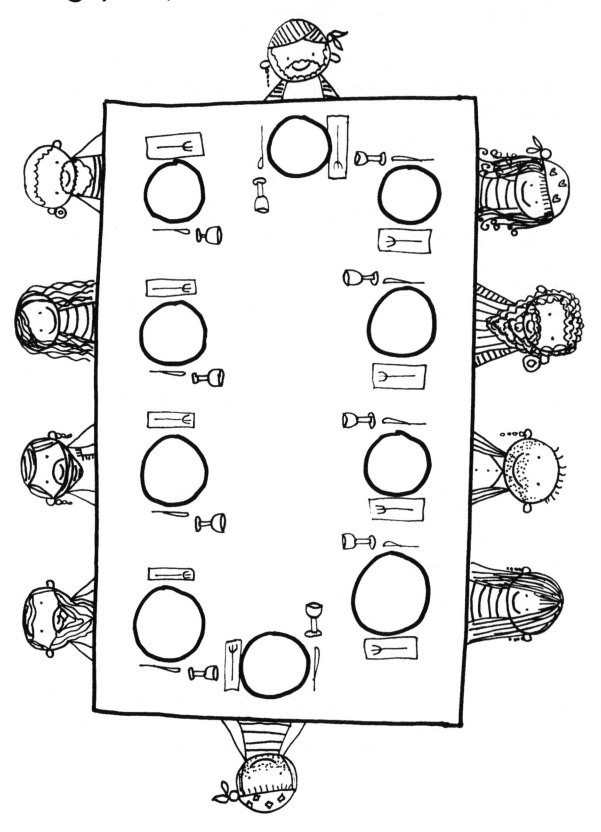

Introduction

You belong to a band of pirates who have been hoping to get ownership of a secret map. The map points the way to a large treasure that was buried on the craggy coast of a far-away island. Someone from the Queen's royal guard is coming to the Captain's quarters to dine with the captain and the pirate crew to discuss a deal. The Queen has agreed that if you and your band of pirates can retrieve the treasure she will let your crew keep half of the fortune. You've got to be on your best behavior for this important event. If you or your pirate friends are too rude or untrustworthy during this dinner meeting, the Queen's guest will break off the deal.

Skill: Giving and receiving compliments

Giving and receiving compliments are important for children to learn because it helps them recognize the good in others as well as accept positive feedback. These skills are not only necessary for building good relationships with others, but also to recognize the good in themselves.

Interventions

THE COMPLIMENT GAME (GROUP VERSION)

The Compliment Game is an activity where children learn to give and receive compliments. It is best done in a group, but as most parents, guardians and counselors only see one or a few children at a time, I have provided an amended version for individual work as well.

To play The Compliment Game, the children sit in a circle. The adult chooses one child to sit in the center or front of the circle. The adult then cues one of the children in the circle to start the game by giving the child in the center a compliment. Eye contact is encouraged but not required. After the compliment, the child in the center says "Thank you" and then turns a little (if necessary) to have better eye contact with the next child. Each child in the circle takes a turn giving a compliment in this way. The child in the center of the circle responds to each compliment by saying "Thank you." When everyone has had a turn giving a compliment, the adult chooses the next child to be in the center of the circle.

Helpful Tips for Playing The Compliment Game

There are some circumstances in which you may need to meet with a child individually before playing the game. This provides an opportunity for the child to have extra support around expectations for the game and to get help with compliments if necessary (e.g. if the child needs assistance coming up with a compliment for a peer they don't get along with). If one of the players is a child who is particularly oppositional or inappropriate, you could help that child think of compliments for each peer and write them out ahead of time. The child can then hand them out during the game instead of saying them. This strategy also works well for children who are shy or nonverbal, and for children who struggle with memory or language barriers. The goal of the game is simply practice—practicing giving and receiving compliments. The more practice the child gets, the more familiar and easier it becomes.

Also, have an adult keep track of the compliments by writing them down for the child. The child will appreciate having a list of these compliments even if they are not reading yet. Children love to share these lists with parents and care providers because it's a boost to their self-esteem and confidence.

A handout of compliments is provided for your convenience. This handout is helpful in providing examples of age-appropriate compliments children can use in the game as well as in interactions with others.

THE COMPLIMENT GAME (INDIVIDUAL VERSION)

Make a list of people in the child's life that they have frequent contact with—siblings, school staff, peers or classmates, the grocery store clerk, a neighbor, etc. They do not need to be people that the child "likes"—they just need to be people the child interacts with on a semi-regular basis.

Help the child come up with a compliment they could give each person on the list. If the child is resistant to the activity, where possible provide a sticker or other reward for each compliment they can come up with.

As for learning to receive compliments, you can role play with the child. Compliment the child and have them practice saying "Thank you" in response.

Compliments

- You are kind to others.

- You draw nice pictures.

- You are fun to be around.

- I appreciate you.

- You're a good listener.

- I look forward to seeing you when I come here.

- I like that you are friendly.

- You're a smart student.

- I feel happy around you.

- You share nicely.

- I've noticed that you're good at…

- I like your smile.

- You are kind to animals.

- You keep your desk clean.

- I like the stories you tell.

- You ask good questions.

- You play fairly.

- You give nice compliments to others.

- You do a great job with…

- You have nice manners.

Skill: Showing kindness

Showing kindness is a skill and character trait that goes a long way in making an impression on others. Encourage your children and/or clients to carry out acts of kindness on a regular basis. This will provide opportunities for the child to receive positive attention, build connections to others, and feel good about themselves. Refer to the Acts of Kindness handout for ways children can show kindness to others.

Acts of Kindness

Regardless of your age, there are many acts of kindness you can do for others! Here are some ideas:

- Smile at someone.

- Do a chore at home without being asked to.

- Call a relative to say hello and/or check in on them.

- Draw or write a kind note for your younger sibling and put it in their coat pocket, lunchbox, or backpack to find later.

- Pick up litter.

- Tell someone you appreciate them.

- Offer to help your teacher with the classroom clean-up.

- Be generous and share.

- Leave a lucky penny (or other good luck charm) for someone to find.

- Hold the door open for someone.

- Make a card for someone and hand deliver it/mail it.

- Give someone a compliment.

- Leave an inspiring quote or message in a magazine at a doctor's office.

- Thank someone for doing their job well.

- Read a book to someone younger than you.

- Write a thank you note or draw a picture for your mail delivery person—leave it in your mailbox for them.

✱

- If you have spare change you can:

    - leave some in a vending machine coin return for someone to find

    - put money in someone's expiring parking meter

    - pay someone's library fine.

- Use chalk to write a positive message for passers-by on the sidewalk or driveway.

- Give a loved one a hug.

- Make a card for your neighbor.

- Add your own ideas here:

_____

_____

_____

_____

_____

_____

_____

_____

_____

_____

_____

_____

Skill: Sharing

Sharing can be a tough skill to teach, and a tough one to learn. Here are some general sharing strategies that may help:

- Put the focus on "taking turns" rather than "sharing."

- If a toddler or young child is playing with an item and another child wants it, communicate the expectations to both children. "Mary is playing with the car now but when she is done with it, you can play with it." Redirect the other child to find something else to play with until Mary is done with her turn.

- Provide a variation of like toys when you know more than one child will be playing (e.g. a variety of toy cars). This way, for example, Mary and her friend have other cars to play with, which encourages both to take turns more easily.

- Children can be encouraged to use other means of play if they are not able to share toys and belongings yet (e.g. take them outside for a nature walk).

- Children can practice taking turns using the toys and games they are less attached to.

- Put the child's most beloved toys or belongings away during play dates.

 # Interventions

THE COOKIE JAR

The Cookie Jar is a brief activity in which the child practices sharing. You can make the jar of pretend cookies yourself. To play the game, give the jar of cookies to the child and ask them to divide the cookies between you both so that each of you has a fair share. This provides an opportunity for the child to practice sharing. As it's a game, and the cookies are not real, the child is less attached to the objects being shared and therefore able to share more easily.

Materials

- Clean jar

- Small blank wood shapes that look like cookies, such as circles, stars, hearts, gingerbread men—you can buy these at a craft shop, or you can cut cookie shapes from recycled cereal or cracker boxes

- Acrylic paints or permanent markers

- Paintbrushes (if using paint)

Directions

- Decorate each of the cookie shapes. You can use swirls for cinnamon cookies, dots for chocolate chip cookies, stripes for fudge striped cookies, multicolored dots for cookies with sprinkles, etc.

- Allow the paint or ink to dry.

- Store the cookies in the jar.

THE TREASURE CHEST

The Treasure Chest is used in the same manner as The Cookie Jar. The treasure chest is filled with treasure pieces that can be equally divided. You and the child can pretend to be pirates who have found this treasure. The child can practice sharing the treasure with you.

Materials

- Small blank wooden treasure chest (found at craft stores)

- Brown and dark brown acrylic paint

- Paintbrush

- Various treasure pieces:

  » Pretend coins—You can make faux coins by cutting out circles from cardboard. Wrap the circles in aluminum foil or color them with metallic paint or pens. School supply shops sell plastic coins for helping children learn to count change, so this is another option if you don't want to make your own.

  » Pretend jewelry—Party supply shops and "dollar stores" are a great place to purchase inexpensive pretend jewelry. Look in the wedding aisle for plastic diamond, gold, or silver rings. In the United States you can look in the Mardi Gras aisle for gold and silver beaded necklaces. If the shop has a pirate themed aisle, all the better!

  » Pretend jewels—Craft shops and "dollar stores" often sell decorative glass or plastic beads, gems, and stones that are placed in vases or used in crafts. I have also used clear diamond-shaped beads and plastic gems to add to the treasure.

Directions

- Paint the treasure chest brown and allow the paint to dry.

- Paint a few horizontal lines along the treasure box using the darker brown. You can also use the darker brown to paint additional hinges or markings on the chest. Allow the paint to dry.

- Add the treasure to the chest.

Note: If you are on a budget with limited time and/or money, re-create this project by turning a paper envelope into the treasure chest and filling it with paper pieces of treasure.

 ## Skill: Winning and losing

It's important for children to learn how to win and lose at games and competitions with a bit of grace. A child who has an outburst after losing a game will quickly alienate their peers, as will gloating about a win.

Provide opportunities for children to play games where they can practice winning and losing. You can help children learn basic skills for playing, winning, and losing by following the recommendations and suggestions in the following handouts.

*

General Game Guidelines for Adults

The following is a list of supportive tips for supervising and/or playing games with children. These suggestions help to reduce the conflict that can occur between younger players.

- Review and agree on the game rules ahead of time—not everybody plays a game by the same rules so it's best to clear this up before you begin.

- Have a discussion prior to the game: "How can someone cheat in this game? What do we do if we see someone cheating?" This discussion sets the tone for fair play. If a child is aware that others in the game are keeping an eye out (and know the signs of) cheating, they are less likely to cheat.

- Before you begin to play, ask the child: "If you start to feel frustrated with the game, what can you do to feel calmer?"

- Create a positive side to losing—for example, make a rule that the winner of the game is the one who has to clean it up and put it away.

- Have stickers or treats that players can earn whenever they say something encouraging during the game or each time they win/lose the game respectfully.

- Check in with players throughout the game as needed: "How is everyone doing? Is anyone feeling frustrated? Does anyone need to take a quick break?"

- Set an example—role model the behaviors you want to see from the players.

- When the game is over, review how it went: "Did anyone have trouble playing respectfully? What did you tell yourself or what did you do during the game to help you when you had to move back 20 spaces or thought you were losing?"

- Provide copies of the Winning and Losing handout for kids who can read so they can refer to it if necessary during the game.

Winning and Losing: Supportive Tips for Kids

During the game:

- Wait your turn.

- Keep your hands to yourself—let others roll their own dice or move their own pieces.

- If you move ahead of other players in the game, do not tease or boast.

- If you fall behind in the game and start to feel upset, remind yourself it's just a game. Take a few deep breaths or take a break.

- Encourage other players by saying things like "Wow! Great job!" or "Good for you!"

If you lose the game:

- Remind yourself that it's just a game and it's okay to lose.

- Tell the other player/s "Good game!"

- Tell the winner "Congratulations!"

- Shake hands or give a "high five" to the winner.

If you win the game:

- Tell the other player/s "Good game!"

- You can feel excited and proud to win the game, but show good sportsmanship—bragging and putting other players down will only make them feel bad and not want to play games with you again.

- Offer to clean up the game.

Write your own suggestions and ideas here:

_____

_____

_____

_____

_____

_____

_____

_____

_____

_____

_____

_____

_____

_____

_____

_____

Skill: Compassion and empathy

Children can learn to feel and show compassion. This is harder to teach to some children than others (for various reasons) but role modeling is key—role model the type of compassion and empathy you want the child to have. You can also volunteer with the child, practice acts of kindness with the child, and read stories about characters facing challenges and adversity followed by discussion about the character's experiences.

 # Interventions

SOMEONE ELSE'S SHOES

Discuss the following with the child:

Have you ever heard the expression "Put yourself in the other person's shoes"? This famous quote means "Try to see it from the other person's point of view." It's about empathy. Empathy is when you try to understand what makes someone react, behave, or appear the way they do. For example, if you were on the subway and you saw a person who looked really tired and they smelled bad, you might find yourself judging that person. You might find yourself thinking, "Yuck! That person smells disgusting!" But rather than judging them, what if you were curious instead? What if you asked yourself: "Why is this person dirty? Why does this person look tired and sad?" What if you asked yourself instead: "How would I want to be treated if I were him?"

Empathy can be a hard skill for some people to learn because it is far easier to judge someone than it is to feel empathy toward them. With some practice though, we can all become more empathic to each other.

Materials

- Scissors

- Pictures or drawings of various shoes and footwear

- Glue

- Index cards or other pieces of paper

Directions

- Cut out various pictures and/or drawings of footwear.

- Glue the images onto the index card or piece of paper—only one image per card.

- Write one of the following scenarios onto each card, or write ones of your own that are more appropriate to your age group and cultural experiences.

- The child who wears these shoes…

  » has to tell his dad that he got in trouble at school today.

  » has her first dance performance on stage tonight.

  » lives with a parent who is sick all the time.

  » was sent home early because she has lice.

  » has never had anyone say "I love you" to her.

  » went to a funeral today.

  » has not eaten in two days.

  » has a brother who was mean to him this morning.

  » lost her favorite stuffed animal.

  » got hit by someone he loves.

  » had a nightmare last night.

  » had an accident in school today.

  » couldn't sleep because of something that happened before bed last night.

  » was teased on the bus this morning.

  » got a bad grade on her test even though she studied.

  » was told by friends to "Go away" at recess.

- Next, allow the cards to dry.

- Have the child pick a card, and read it to them if necessary. Ask the child: "How do you think the child in this situation feels?" You can also ask: "Is there anything you could do in this situation to help the person? If you can't think of any way to help, what is something you could do to not make their day worse?"

CRUMPLED PAPER HEART

The Crumpled Paper Heart has become a common activity in classrooms to show children the impact of being unkind to others. The crumpled heart is a visual metaphor for how words and actions can leave an imprint on someone's heart.

Directions

- Cut a large heart out of paper.

- Ask the child: "How do you think someone's heart feels when someone says something unkind?" You can paraphrase or suggest that when this has happened to you, your heart felt crumpled.

- Next, ask the child (or children) to list some unkind things that kids say to each other, or have said to them. For each answer, crumple a section of the heart.

- When they have listed all they can think of, look at the heart and note how crumpled it looks.

- Next, discuss the following: "What are some things people do when they are sorry that they hurt someone's feelings?" Some examples are: "They say they're sorry" or "They make up." You can suggest that apologizing and making amends is a way we try to "un-crumple" someone's heart when we have hurt it.

- Now flatten the heart out as best you can.

- Ask the child: "Is the heart the same as it was before?"

- The child will usually note that the heart still has wrinkles in it or has a few rips. You can use this as an example or metaphor that when we act unkind toward others, we can't take back what we said or did—we can only apologize and try to make the situation right. Our words and actions can leave a lasting impression on others and therefore, we need to treat each other with kindness and respect.

 # Skill: Apologizing

Children make mistakes, as we all do. Apologizing is an important social skill to have. When a child feels confident in knowing how to say they are sorry and to make amends quickly, they (and the people they hurt) can move forward and not get bogged down in unhealthy behaviors. These unhealthy behaviors include: avoidance—avoiding the person they upset (in place of saying they are sorry), feeling shame for what they have done (because they haven't had resolution), and denying they did anything hurtful (creating a defense mechanism). The earlier we teach children to apologize in a meaningful manner, the healthier their relationships and self-confidence can be.

Parents and care providers can help children learn the skills to apologize via role modeling (i.e. say you are sorry to your kids or clients when you make a mistake or have been unfair or grumpy with them), via role playing (practice with them), and via rewarding your child when they do apologize. This can be as simple as noticing they apologized and giving them verbal praise for doing so.

 ## Intervention

PUPPET APOLOGIES

Puppet Apologies is an activity where you and the child role play various scenarios in which a character needs to apologize for something. For this activity I've included some puppet characters and scenarios (Puppet Apology Cards). You and the child take turns drawing a card and then use the finger puppets to show how the character could apologize and/or make amends. Each scenario uses two characters—you can either role play one of the characters and have the child role play the other, or each player can act out both roles when it is their turn.

Materials

- Finger puppet sheets and Puppet Apology Cards
- Glue
- Thin cardboard (e.g. a recycled cereal box or cardstock)
- Scissors

Directions

- Color the finger puppet characters.
- Glue the page/s onto thin cardboard.
- Cut the puppets out.
- Cut out the circles as indicated by the dotted lines—this is where you place your fingers. Your fingers become the character's legs.
- Next, cut out the cards provided for Puppet Apologies. You and the child take turns drawing a card and then role playing ways to apologize or make amends in each situation. The scenarios are humorous and exaggerated to appeal to children and to make the practice enjoyable. There are four characters in Puppet Apologies: a Queen, a Cat, a Unicorn, and a Pickle Slice.

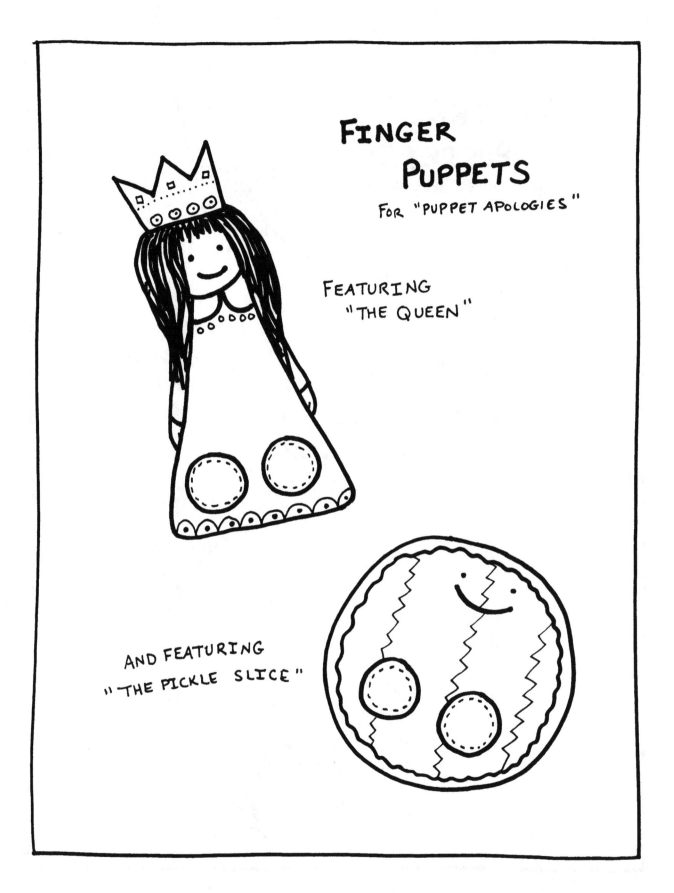

FINGER PUPPETS
FOR "PUPPET APOLOGIES"

FEATURING "THE QUEEN"

AND FEATURING "THE PICKLE SLICE"

FINGER PUPPETS
FOR "PUPPET APOLOGIES"

FEATURING "THE UNICORN"

AND FEATURING "THE CAT"

Puppet Apology Cards

The Queen told the Cat: "I hope you eat a rotten fish."

The Cat got angry and tossed a fishbone at the Queen. It hit her on the crown!

The Cat told the Pickle Slice: "You stink!"

The Pickle Slice spit vinegar on the Unicorn.

The Queen spread a rumor about the Pickle Slice.

The Unicorn pushed the Pickle Slice.

The Queen cut in front of the Pickle Slice in line.

The Cat said hello to the Unicorn, but the Unicorn ignored him.

*

The Unicorn told the Pickle Slice that nobody likes him.

The Queen told the Cat that she is better than he is.

The Unicorn brought rainbows to all of her friends, except the Cat.

The Pickle Slice blamed something on the Queen. He told everyone the Queen made a mess when it was the Pickle Slice who did it.

The Unicorn asked the Queen to play with her at recess. The Queen said she would. But when recess came, the Queen went and played with someone else.

The Cat stayed on the swing the entire recess and did not give the Unicorn a turn.

The Queen made noises on purpose to make the Cat annoyed.

WRITTEN APOLOGY NOTES

Kids often make mistakes and then don't know how to deal with the situation. Written Apology Notes (see handout) are a simple but meaningful way for the child to communicate to someone else that they are sorry. Cut the notes apart and then store them where children can access them as needed.

Skill: Expressing gratitude and saying "Thank you"

Another skill that children need to learn is gratitude and expressing thanks. When other people go out of their way to give you their time, money, and/or gifts it's important to say thank you and express gratitude. Sometimes it's helpful to remind children that the more they express gratitude, the more abundance they will have in their lives because people are more giving and generous to those who show gratitude and appreciation.

Intervention

THANK YOU NOTES

Photocopy the Thank You Note and have the child decorate and/or color it. Help the child identify someone they can thank. It can be as simple as thanking someone for a gift, or thanking someone for a smile or a word of encouragement. Like apologizing, the best way for children to become better at saying "Thank you" is to see you doing it (role modeling), to role play situations in which the child can practice saying "Thank you," and to provide the opportunities for the child to express their thanks.

*

To: _____
From: _____

I AM SO SORRY THAT
I _____
_____
_____

I'M SORRY!

I MADE A MISTAKE.
I AM SORRY THAT I
_____
_____
_____

I'M SORRY!

To: _____
From: _____

To: _____
From: _____

I'M SORRY!

I DID NOT MEAN TO
_____
_____

I AM SO SORRY THAT
I DID THAT.

I'M VERY SORRY THAT
I _____
_____
_____
_____

To: _____
From: _____

To: _____

Thank You!!

I am thanking you for: _____
_____
_____

because: _____
_____
_____.

That was very thoughtful of you and I appreciate it!

From: _____

An accompanying story

Fahim and the Camel

Fahim lived in the desert. There was a tradition in Fahim's village that older children were allowed to have their own camel when they became responsible enough to care for one. Well, Fahim had just been given his first camel and he couldn't wait to ride it into the village to show his friends! He was so proud and excited!

Fahim's camel was a challenge, however. When Fahim got close to the camel, it would spit at him. When Fahim tried to talk to the camel, it would turn away from him and ignore him. And whenever Fahim brought other camels and friends around, the camel would act grumpy and rude to the others.

Fahim was very sad that his camel was acting so rude and unkind.

One day Fahim's aunt stopped by with her own camel. She told Fahim and his family that she needed them to take care of her camel, just for a little while. She was going on a sea journey and she couldn't bring the camel with her.

Fahim said he would take good care of the camel. And each day Fahim really did look after it well. He fed it, brushed it, and talked to it. He was even able to start riding it to the village market. Each time the camel brought Fahim to the market and back, Fahim gave the camel a treat. Fahim would tell the camel nice things and scratch it behind the ears (which camels like). Fahim and his aunt's camel quickly became good companions.

Fahim's own camel took notice of how much fun Fahim was having with the other camel. The other camel was more polite and gentle with Fahim; it was more approachable and easier to ride because it listened to him; and the local children loved to come and visit the aunt's camel because it was friendly and had nice manners.

Fahim's camel then realized how rude and unkind it had been to Fahim and the other children. It didn't want to be rude and unkind. It didn't want to be thought of as mean and unfriendly. It wanted to be liked by Fahim and the children. So Fahim's camel started to act more gentle and polite with the boy and his friends. It started to greet them whenever they came near. It stopped spitting and being rude. The more it got to know Fahim, the more it realized how much happier it was to have a friend.

The camel could not speak but it did try to show Fahim how sorry it was for being difficult to get along with. Fahim and his camel started to become good friends and, sure enough, Fahim started riding his camel to the market and everywhere else. The camel now got lots of praise, attention, and treats—and it liked that! Fahim liked it too!

An activity to go along with the story

MAKE A CLOTHESPIN CAMEL

Materials

- The camel coloring sheet
- Coloring pens/crayons
- Scissors
- 2 clothespins for each camel

Directions

- Optional: Choose an affirmation from below and write it on the camel's blanket.
- Color the camel and then cut it out.
- Attach the clothespins to the camel for legs.

✓ Affirmations

- ✓ I am kind to others.
- ✓ I am a good friend.
- ✓ I appreciate kindness.

MAKE A "CLOTHESPIN CAMEL"

Color and decorate your camel and then cut it out!

Attach your clothespins here!

CHAPTER 2

Creating Healthy Boundaries

. . . .

 ## Challenges

The child has inappropriate boundaries.

The child approaches strangers and/or treats strangers the same as family and friends.

The child doesn't know own strength and is too rough with others.

 ## Goals

The child will have appropriate boundaries with others.

The child will not be approaching and/or hugging strangers.

The child will keep their hands to themself.

 ## Skill: Honoring personal space

Some children are more intuitive and observant than others when it comes to understanding and honoring people's personal space. For those who struggle with this, there are various ways to educate them about this societal and cultural norm, as well as ways to practice it.

 Interventions

HULA HOOP ZONES

Materials

- A hula hoop

Directions

- Have the child hold a hula hoop around them so that they are in the center of it.

- Point out that the hula hoop creates a zone around the child, and that this represents personal space.

You can describe the concept of personal space by stating that the zone inside the hula hoop is a "space bubble"—it's the amount of space the child should allow between themself and others in most social situations. Some kids will ask why space bubbles are so important. You can answer them that most people feel uncomfortable when others stand too close to them, and some people think it's very rude to stand too close to others. If we want people to feel safe and comfortable next to us, we need to honor people's need for personal space.

Note: The amount of space that is socially acceptable is highly dependent on the child's culture, so space bubbles can be wider or smaller depending on the social norms of the child's family and culture.

Brainstorm the following with the child:

Sometimes there are moments when it's okay to be in someone's space bubble. These times include standing in line, riding on a crowded subway, or standing in an elevator. Can you think of some other times when it might be okay to stand close to someone for just a little bit?

SPACE BUBBLE DETECTIVES

Space Bubble Detectives is an activity where children practice observing verbal and nonverbal cues regarding personal space. Use the Space Bubble Cues handout before the activity, if needed, to review and discuss how to recognize cues regarding personal space. Then, head out to a public or community space to see if you can find anyone expressing or showing such cues.

Materials

- Clipboard or notebook

- Pencil

- Detective-inspired costume props (optional)

Directions

- Walk around a public or community space with the child and have the child observe people interacting with each other. The child can draw an observation or make a note whenever they see people displaying cues around personal space. For example:

  » "The woman went to hug the girl and the girl didn't look comfortable— I don't think the girl wanted a hug."

  » "The boy went over to the other boy and grabbed a truck out of his hands. The other boy cried and got angry."

- To make the activity more fun you can always offer a small treat or sticker for each observation the child records or reports.

Note: If you are a care provider, such as a counselor, and you cannot logistically do this activity with the child, ask the parent or guardian to play Space Bubble Detectives at home with the parent or guardian leading the activity.

Space Bubble Cues

How do you know if you are getting too close to someone's personal space? Here are some cues to look for:

- The person takes a step back.

- The person tilts their head down.

- The person looks uncomfortable.

- The person says, "You're standing too close," or asks you to back up.

What other cues do you notice? Write them here:

_____

_____

_____

_____

_____

_____

And how do you know when someone is getting too close to *your* space bubble? Tick whichever one/s apply to you.

☐ You feel like backing up or moving away.

☐ You get an icky feeling in your tummy.

☐ You feel uncomfortable.

☐ You don't like that person being so close to you.

What are other things you do or feel when someone is standing too close to you? Write them here:

_____

_____

_____

_____

_____

_____

If someone is standing too close to you, you can try one or more of these things:

- Step back or move away to create a more comfortable amount of space.

- If that person steps into your space bubble again, use words to tell them they are standing too close and that it's making you feel uncomfortable.

- If the person does not give you more space, walk away and tell a trusted grown-up what is going on.

- If that grown-up does not listen, stay away from the person who is making you feel uncomfortable.

- If you have other suggestions or ideas, write them here:

_____

_____

_____

_____

_____

_____

CARPET SQUARES

If you do any floor activities with a group of children, you can use carpet squares to show where each child should be sitting on the floor. The carpet squares create a visual for each child to "see" how close they should be sitting together. Velcro strips or rubber mats can be applied to the bottom of the squares to help them stay in place. If carpet squares are not available, you can use masking tape or paint to mark the spaces instead.

MY HUG BOOK

A Hug Book is a book that is made for a child to show who is okay for that child to hug. These books are especially helpful for children who tend to approach and/or hug anyone and everyone. The book can be as simple as a few pieces of paper folded in half with photos of loved ones inside.

Refer to the book often—a child with poor boundaries needs many reminders to respect their own and others' personal space. For example, read the book frequently so the child can name who is in the Hug Book. Before you go into a store or new place, cue your child ahead of time that they are not to go up to people unless they are in the Hug Book.

APPROPRIATE SENSORY SEEKING

Some children are more hands on or rough with others. Sometimes this is due to a child's need and/or desire for more intensive sensory input. If your child needs added outlets to meet their sensory needs, refer to the handout Appropriate Sensory Seeking for Children. In some cases, when a child gets plenty of sensory input, they become better able to keep their hands to themself.

Appropriate Sensory Seeking for Children

- Offer snacks and meals that provide sensory input—foods that are crispy, chunky, spicy, cold, hot, or crunchy. Provide a straw, or even a spoon, for drinks.

- Offer books that have vivid illustrations, multiple fonts, added textures, or pop-up features.

- Let the child experiment with music by playing various instruments (including simple handmade ones), dancing to music, and listening to a variety of sound and music styles.

- Choose clothing that has textures such as corduroy or flannel, mixed with features such as buttons and collars. You can also sew a piece of corduroy or Velcro inside a child's pocket or at the bottom of a shirt so they can fidget with it.

- Get or make a weighted blanket for your child.

- Replace the child's seat with a yoga ball or wiggly seat.

- Provide plenty of physical activity for the child.

- Get the child outdoors as often as possible.

- Play with clay, play dough, and other materials that encourage squishing, molding, pounding, and manipulating.

- Make a collection of "fidgets" (see page 58). Put them in a basket or bin where the child can access them when needed.

- Provide opportunities for the child to experience swinging and/or spinning (i.e. merry-go-round).

✱

- Add your own ideas and suggestions here:

_____

_____

_____

_____

_____

_____

_____

_____

_____

_____

_____

_____

_____

_____

_____

_____

_____

BLOWING AND CATCHING BUBBLES

Blowing bubbles is an opportunity to practice control, self-regulation, and boundaries. Try blowing bubbles with the child and prompt them to try some or all of these mini-challenges.

Materials

- Small container of bubble liquid

- Bubble wand

Mini challenges

- Touch a bubble without popping it.

- Catch a bubble on your bubble wand.

- Catch a bubble in your hand without it popping.

- Catch a bubble on your nose without it popping.

- Show me what happens when you blow a bubble using gentle breath.

- Show me what happens when you blow a bubble using a strong forceful breath.

- Try and make the biggest bubble that you can. What helped you to make a big bubble? What got in the way of making a big bubble?

- Try and make the smallest bubble that you can.

Blowing bubbles in this manner is not only good practice in building skills for self-control and boundaries, but it is also a helpful reference point to bring up with the child when they are struggling with a boundary issue. For example, if the child is being too hands on with another child, you can remind them: "Remember that time we played with bubbles and we had to be super gentle if we wanted to play with the bubbles, otherwise they would pop? Well, your friends are like bubbles—you need to either leave them alone or be super gentle with them if you want them to stay around you."

USE STORE-BOUGHT GAMES

Jenga®, Pick Up Sticks®, and Operation® are a few of the many games on the market that encourage strategic gentleness to win the game. If the child needs practice being gentle and staying in control of their body and boundaries, these games can provide some practice for building these skills.

BUILD A CARD HOUSE

Building "houses" out of playing cards requires a great degree of patience and self-control. Like blowing bubbles, playing Jenga®, or playing Pick Up Sticks®, it's an opportunity to practice self-control and boundaries. One way to succeed in building card houses is to be mindful of your space (e.g. if you bump into one card, even a little bit, the whole card house will collapse, so it's best to move slow and steady).

The general concept of building card houses is that you frame and lean cards into pyramids and boxes, also called "card houses." A carpeted floor can make this activity easier, as can a floor with many cracks or spaces between floor boards. However, if you are building card houses with younger children, you might want to cut slits into some of the cards to aid in building. You can cut slits about 1 in (2.54 cm) deep at the center of each card (1–4 slits per playing card).

MAKE DOMINO TRAILS

Materials

- One or more sets of dominoes

Directions

- To create a domino trail you will need to make a line of dominoes that are placed vertically next to each other, and evenly spaced about ¼ in (6 mm) apart from the next one in line. You can curve your domino tracks by slightly turning each domino as you go.

- When you build domino tracks, you are practicing self-control and boundaries—if you bump into any dominoes within the track, they will all cascade and collapse. So, you must be very mindful of your body and the dominoes as you build the track.

- Once you have used all the dominoes or have built the track you want, gently tap the first or last domino in line and then all the other dominos will follow.

Helpful suggestion: Place blocks or objects between sections of the track if you or the child is especially prone to bumping the dominoes. This will ensure that only sections of the trail collapse, rather than the entire trail.

 ## An accompanying story

Basil the Billy Goat

Basil was a playful goat who loved to jump and run. His favorite part of the school day was playing at recess. His favorite part of his time at home was playing in the yard with his neighbors.

But even though Basil loved to play, he had trouble making and keeping friends because he was too rough or rude, without even meaning to be. Basil was usually trying to help someone out or trying to cheer someone up, but this only seemed to get him in trouble. For example, one time Basil went to a birthday party. The birthday goat was too shy to open presents in front of everybody, so Basil started opening the presents for his friend to help his friend out. This did not go down well at all—the birthday goat became very upset.

At the same party, Basil was first in line to hit the *piñata* with a stick. Basil thought he was being helpful by breaking the *piñata* open, but instead the other goats were upset because they didn't get a turn to hit the *piñata*.

On another day, Basil went to the park and spun the merry-go-round so fast that one of the goats fell off and got hurt. Then Basil pushed a little goat on the swing but pushed too hard and the goat fell off. It seemed like Basil was always getting in trouble for being too rough or pushy. Basil never did these things on purpose to hurt anyone or hurt their feelings—they just happened!

Basil's mom sat down with Basil. She said she noticed how hard it was for Basil to keep his hands to himself and be gentle with others. She wondered out loud if maybe Basil needed more activity in his life to help him get that energy out. She also wondered if he needed more practice in being gentler, too. Basil and his mom made a plan—the plan was that his mom would make sure Basil got more activity in the day and that Basil would use some tricks to help him keep his hands to himself. One of these tricks was a bead that Basil kept in his pocket—whenever he felt like squeezing, grabbing, or holding something, he would do that to his bead.

Mom and Basil decided that after a while, if Basil was still being too rough, they would look for added support or help. Basil's mom said sometimes "occupational therapy" or other therapies could help little goats feel more in control of their bodies. Basil felt better having a plan because he was willing to do anything to make and keep friends and feel more in control of his body.

 ## An activity to go along with the story

PICK A BEAD

Have a small bowl of beads available in your office or home and let the child choose a bead to use during an activity with you, such as playing a board game. The child can practice using the bead as a "fidget"—a fidget is an object used for holding and/ or manipulating. Fidgets also redirect a person's need for movement and sensory input to the fidget instead of other people and objects.

Prior to using the bead as a fidget, remind the child that the bead is to stay in the child's pocket or hand. If the bead gets thrown, rolled away, or in any other way misused, then this intervention is not helping the child. However, if the child uses the bead appropriately under supervision, you can let them try it somewhere else. Taking the bead outside of your office or home is an earned privilege because it shows the child has been responsible with it so far.

✔ Affirmations

✔ Hands to myself.

✔ I am gentle.

✔ Give others space.

CHAPTER 3

Reducing Oppositional Behavior

. . . .

 ## Challenges

The child doesn't do as I ask.

The child insists on doing things their way.

 ## Goal

The child will follow directions after 1–2 prompts.

 ## Skill: Following directions

In many cultures children are expected to listen to their elders and follow directions. But it's probably safe to say we've all had a child in our lives—at some point—who did not want to do so. Anyone who has been in a power struggle with a toddler or child knows how exhausting and frustrating it can be for all involved. Some of the time these behaviors are rooted in normal childhood development (i.e. the child is going through an age-appropriate developmental stage where it's the child's job to push limits and practice being more independent). But sometimes the child may be oppositional for other reasons.

The child could be an experiential learner. Experiential learners learn by doing—not by hearing. For example, you can tell an experiential learner that if they go outside in the snow without mittens, their hands will get cold. The child might protest and therefore come across as defiant, but telling this child is not the most helpful way for them to learn. In a case like this, as long as the child is not going to get hurt, you have an opportunity to let them figure out the natural consequences on their own. If they put up a struggle about wearing mittens, disengage from the struggle and keep mittens on hand for when/ if they ask for them. Once a child learns from the experience on their own, they are more likely to understand you when you suggest wearing mittens next time, because now they have experienced what happens when they play in the snow without them.

Another group of children that can come across as oppositional are those who were neglected and/or left on their own to care and fend for themselves. In an ideal world all children would be raised with love and nurturing, but as we know in the counseling field, various forms of neglect happen all too frequently. Some parents have drug and alcohol addictions, others might have a severe mental illness, and some may lack empathy or parental instincts. The end result is a child raising themselves either full or part time. It can be challenging to set limits and give directions to such children because they are so used to figuring things out on their own and making their own decisions. These children can come across as being oppositional when really they have not had the opportunity to be children and trust adults to care for them or tell them what to do.

In addition, some children have hearing difficulty, speech and language challenges, or other factors that contribute to coming across as "not listening."

Regardless of the reason behind the child's behavior, there are ways to encourage a child to do as you ask, and to follow your directions.

 ## Interventions

CREATE A REWARD SYSTEM

A reward system means you provide rewards for positive behaviors. Rather than focusing on what you DON'T want your child to be doing, you focus on what you DO want them to be doing. Reward systems include behavior and incentive charts, sticker charts, and earned privileges.

Rewarding Puzzles

Purchase or make a simple jigsaw puzzle—about 10–24 pieces. Glue magnet strips onto the back of each puzzle piece. Each time your child shows the positive behavior you are encouraging (i.e. each time your child complies with doing a task or each time your child responds with appropriate words instead of having a tantrum, etc.), they earn a puzzle piece. They can display the puzzle pieces on the refrigerator or other metal surface. When the child earns all the puzzle pieces, they can complete the puzzle (or you can do it together) and the child earns a reward.

Spell it Out

Buy one or more sets of plastic magnetic alphabet letters so you can spell out the reward your child is working toward. If you are on a budget, you can always choose the word "PRIZE," which requires only one set of magnetic letters. Each time your child does the positive behavior you are encouraging, they earn the next letter in the word. When the whole word is spelled out, the child receives their prize.

Community Reinforcement

When my son was a toddler I started using Community Reinforcement as a way to recognize and reward his positive behaviors in the community. Our deal was this: each time we left the house to run errands, attend appointments, or do any other activity in the community, he earned an inexpensive reward for each and every compliment that someone gave him about his positive behaviors, manners, or kindness. The compliments often came from strangers who noticed his patience in the grocery aisle line, or opening the door for someone else. Sometimes the compliments came from other parents we knew or teachers at his school. Regardless of who the compliments came from, I honored each and every one with a token of appreciation to my child (e.g. an inexpensive toy or a treat). This can be a simple way to encourage your child to follow directions and be respectful.

Incentive Charts

An incentive chart is a chart that identifies the positive behavior you are encouraging, as well as how many times the behavior needs to be carried out before the incentive is earned. A simple chart might have a statement across the top, such as "When Ellie cleans her room ten times *without arguing* she will earn a trip to the ice cream shop." The chart might then have ten boxes to check off each time Ellie complies with cleaning her room without arguing. You can also use the Incentive Charts provided as a handout.

Simple Incentive Charts

EACH TIME I _____,
I CAN COLOR IN A **TREE**.
WHEN THEY ARE ALL EARNED AND
COLORED I CAN HAVE THIS:

EACH TIME I _____,
I CAN COLOR IN A **VEGETABLE**.
WHEN THEY ARE ALL EARNED AND
COLORED I CAN HAVE THIS:

EACH TIME I _____,
I CAN COLOR IN A **KITTEN**.
WHEN THEY ARE ALL EARNED AND
COLORED I CAN HAVE THIS:

EACH TIME I _____,
I CAN COLOR IN AN **INSECT**.
WHEN THEY ARE ALL EARNED AND
COLORED I CAN HAVE THIS:

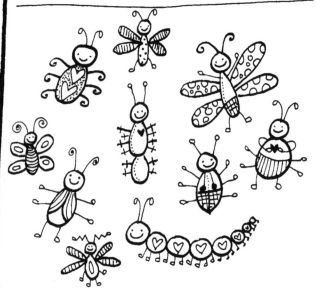

NATURAL CONSEQUENCES

Some children learn best from natural consequences rather than punishment or rewards. If your child tends to act out when you ask them to do something reasonable, then specific communication about your expectations and the consequences for not following through might be helpful.

For example, you are going to the grocery store with your daughter to pick up an item for dinner. Your daughter tends to ask you to buy her something whenever she goes in the store, and then have an outburst when you tell her no. In this situation, you could communicate the expectations and consequences with the following in mind:

- *Communicate the expectations:* Before going in the store, define what you are there for. If you have extra money for your daughter to get a treat, let her know the maximum amount she can spend. If you do not have extra money for her to get a treat, let her know ahead of time.

- *Communicate the consequences:* Define what the consequences will be if she has a tantrum and/or becomes disrespectful in the store.

- *Remind her of the coping strategies to use if she becomes frustrated.*

If she does well in the store, she earns the privilege of going to the store with you next time.

If she ends up having a tantrum or being disrespectful, the natural consequence would be that she does not go to the store with you next time, in addition to any other consequences you established (e.g. she will not be going to her friend's house to play later, either).

A counselor or other provider might also use natural consequences.

For example, you've probably experienced a session where you've set a limit or expectation with a client and then that client refused to comply (or was not able to comply for other reasons).

Let's say you decide to do sand tray therapy with a client today. When the young client comes to the session, you inform him you'll be doing your first sand tray activity with him. You communicate your expectations by going over the basic and reasonable rules of the activity (e.g. the sand stays in the tray).

During the session the boy gets excited playing in the sand and starts to smash and crash cars in the tray, which causes sand to spill over. You redirect him and remind him that the sand needs to stay in the tray. The boy becomes oppositional—he purposefully picks up a handful of sand and throws it. You handle the situation as you need to, but the ultimate natural consequence is that the sand tray is not offered again until the child is able to follow the rules.

Next week, the boy asks to use the sand tray. You reply that the activity will not be an option again until he can use the sand tray respectfully.

You might be wondering how you can know when a child is able to follow through with limits the next time. Here are some considerations:

- The child accepts the consequence respectfully.

- The child is able to reflect on the behavior and understand the consequence.

- The child is willing to role play an appropriate way they could have handled the situation.

- The child has practiced more calming and coping skills since the last opportunity or session.

- The child shows you concerted effort to follow limits more respectfully.

DRAW THIS!

Draw This! is an explorative and hands on way to practice giving and following directions. You and the child take turns drawing objects and animals based on the directions you are given by each other. For example:

- door
- car
- mountain
- tree
- cloud
- balloon
- bird
- cookie
- heart
- stick figure person
- slice of watermelon
- dog

- cat
- ladder
- window
- slice of cheese
- flower
- starfish
- house
- football
- slice of pizza
- rabbit
- fish
- sun

Materials

- Scrap paper
- Pencil

Directions

- Player 1 tries to get Player 2 to draw an object or animal without labeling or naming the object being drawn. Therefore, Player 1 has to describe specific directions for various lines and shapes for Player 2 to draw. Here is an example:

    Player 1 tries to get Player 2 to draw an apple.

    Player 1: "Draw a circle—the circle doesn't have to be perfectly round. When you are done drawing the circle, draw a little line coming up from the top of the circle."

- You can play as many rounds as you like.

- Have a follow-up discussion about what it's like to play this game. You can use the following questions:

    Is it easier to give the instructions or to follow them?

    Was any part of this game frustrating?

    What did you need from the other player while you were drawing?

    What did you need from the other player while you were giving directions?

Variations

Player 1 can either watch Player 2 drawing (allowing Player 1 to give more specific directions), or have Player 2 draw the entire picture as directed, only revealing the drawing at the end.

DICE SOLUTIONS

When you have a strong-willed child, a set of dice can be of help. As many power struggles come from a child wanting control of a situation, dice can be a moderator between the parent and child. Here are some examples of ways to use dice:

- *Your child is having trouble transitioning from one activity to the next:* Have the child roll the dice. The number rolled on the dice is how many more minutes the child has before the activity is over.

- *Your child does not want to eat any more dinner, but you want them to take a few more bites:* The child rolls the dice to see how many more bites they need before they can have dessert.

- *The child wants to stay up a few more minutes before going to bed:* Have the child roll the dice to find out how many more minutes they can stay up before bed.

In each situation, the power struggle is reduced because the dice is deciding. This is best used as a once or twice a day activity so that the child is still learning to follow limits through the rest of the day. But for those particularly tough moments that seem to be the same power struggle each and every day, using dice may help to break the pattern of opposition and give the child a chance to feel in control.

IT'S ON THE WALL

Have an area in your living space where daily or weekly responsibilities are clearly defined for each child and posted on the wall. A bulletin board, a corkboard, and posters can help you organize this information. The information can include a specific schedule for each day of the week, chores that need to be done and who is responsible for them, as well as family and household rules such as "no hitting," "no jumping on the couch," etc.

Once everything is "On the Wall," you will find that power struggles can decrease. Children who are oppositional or defiant can be especially skilled at pushing limits, so the more you can define what's expected, the easier it is to hold your ground when the child is trying to take advantage. If your child tries to renegotiate or test limits, you can give them a consistent response: "Let's go check the wall and see what we decided about that already," or "Go check the wall and see what it says about that." If you remain consistent in your responses your child eventually learns that those limits and expectations are not negotiable.

You may find some of those items listed on the wall need to be written more specifically over time, especially if your child is a master at trying to get around limits or rules. In addition, it's also helpful to have a ring binder in which each household chore is listed on a separate sheet of paper and the chore is defined and listed in steps. If you can laminate these instruction sheets, that's even better. I once worked in a group home where the teens were especially adept at finding a way around limits and rules. When it was time to get their chores done, however, there was little argument because the chore sheets were so specific. There were no more power struggles around "You said to clean my room—my room is clean!" because now "clean" was clearly defined.

WAIT... DID YOU JUST SAY, "YES"?

This intervention works best with younger children who find exaggeration funny. The gist of this intervention is that every time your child says "yes," "okay," and/or complies with what you asked, you respond happily in an exaggerated and dramatic manner. Make a ridiculous facial expression…fall to the floor…pretend some beautiful magic just happened in your home…pretend you must be dreaming…etc. Children love having humorous and silly moments with their parents, so this intervention might be a way to encourage your child to continue to do as you asked. Not all children appreciate exaggeration (my son rarely did, so this was not an intervention that worked for us), but if you have a kid who loves silliness or drama, this intervention may be one to try.

 ## An accompanying story
Sir Refuses-a-Lot

Sir Refuses-a-Lot was a knight who often got himself into trouble for not following directions. It seemed no matter how many times the Queen gave Sir Refuses-a-Lot a direction or command, he decided to do it his own way instead.

Well, the Queen had a very important message to deliver to the royal family in the neighboring kingdom. All of the Queen's messengers were away on errands. Sir Refuses-a-Lot was pacing in the courtyard and the Queen hesitated about giving him such a very important job. But she was desperate to get this message out, and she didn't have time to do it herself. She took a deep breath and said to Sir Refuses-a-Lot: "I have this very important message for you to deliver. It must arrive at the neighboring kingdom by sunset. Can I trust you to deliver this message by then?"

Sir Refuses-a-Lot gave a groan and a sigh. He didn't want to deliver this message—the roads between their castle and the neighboring kingdom were dusty and full of rocks and potholes. Sir Refuses-a-Lot preferred the smoother grass roads in the countryside. But the Queen handed him the message and said: "Please, Sir Refuses-a-Lot, please get this message delivered on time."

As Sir Refuses-a-Lot was packing his satchel for the trip, the Queen reminded him to stay on the dirt road as that was the fastest route for him to travel.

Sir Refuses-a-Lot and his horse set off to deliver the message. The horse galloped along the dusty roads at a good speed, but Sir Refuses-a-Lot noticed his clothing was getting covered in dust. He didn't like that one bit, so at the next crossroads, he decided to travel a part of the journey on the grass road instead. "I'm going to do this my way!" he said.

But the grass road ended up being a little tricky because his horse kept stopping to eat the grass. "Oh fiddlesticks!" said Sir Refuses-a-Lot. "We'll just go back to the dirt road after all!"

The knight and his horse trotted along the dirt road until they came up behind a caravan. It was a very slow-moving caravan and very large, too! There was no room on the road to pass it. Sir Refuses-a-Lot became annoyed and grumbled to his horse to make a shortcut through the forest. "I'm going to do this my way!" he said.

But soon, Sir Refuses-a-Lot realized they were lost. Making a short cut through the forest was not a good idea after all. The knight told his horse to turn around and follow their tracks back to the dirt road.

"Okay, horse," he said, "we can still make it to the neighboring kingdom by sunset if we go very VERY fast!" So the horse started to gallop.

The knight noticed the sun was no longer overhead and it was starting to lower toward the horizon. He had a moment of panic, thinking he might not deliver the message in time, so he looked around for a faster way to get there.

They came upon a dark pathway that seemed to veer directly toward the neighboring kingdom's castle. He could just see the castle tops from where they were now. "I bet if we took this other path, we could get to the castle sooner! So…I'm going to do this my way!" he said.

The knight and the horse headed up the dark pathway. "Nope, nope, nope, nope…never mind!" the knight whispered under his breath. There was a giant slimy dragon asleep in the center of that darkened path! There was no way that knight was going to try and sneak past it. So, back to the dusty dirt road they went.

Well, needless to say, the sun set before the knight was able to deliver the message. He had failed the Queen. As a result, she took away his knightly privileges and demoted him to a stable helper where his only companion was the former Sir Argues-a-Lot. Both of these former knights were given back their common names, Bob and Ted, and they spent the rest of their days cleaning up after the horses and grumbling at each other.

 ## An activity to go along with the story

MAKE A SIR REFUSES-A-LOT

Color Sir Refuses-a-Lot on the activity page and then cut him out. Each time the child notices that Sir Refuses-a-Lot is not following the Queen's directions, or each time he says, "I'm going to do it my way!" the child can wave his Sir Refuses-a-Lot in the air.

 ## Affirmations

✔ Yes.

✔ Okay!

✔ I will try.

✔ I can do this.

Sir Refuses-a-Lot :

① Color Sir Refuses-a-Lot and cut him out

② Listen to the story about Sir Refuses-a-Lot

③ Every time you hear Sir Refuses-a-Lot saying "I'll do it my way!", or not following the Queen's orders, wave your Sir Refuses-a-Lot in the air!

Sir Refuses-a-Lot

CHAPTER 4

Anger Management

· ·

Challenges

The child gets frustrated and irritable easily.

The child does not have the skills yet to manage their anger.

Goals

The child will identify what triggers their frustration.

The child will try at least three new calming/coping strategies.

The child will have the coping skills to diffuse their anger and calm themselves.

Skill: Anger management

In this chapter you will find a variety of opportunities to practice skills in anger management including recognizing triggers, practicing and rating calming interventions, breathing, using physical means for releasing tension, and creating safety zones and quiet spaces for calming.

✚ Interventions

BRAINSTORMING SESSION: WHAT'S FRUSTRATING?

Have a brainstorming session with the child about what triggers their frustration. The child might be able to identify certain triggers such as "I get mad when…my sister tells me what to do," or "I feel upset when…the kids at the playground tell me I can't play kickball." These triggers are helpful to identify, when possible, so you can prompt the child to use their coping strategies when these events happen, or even before they happen (e.g. "We are going to the park in ten minutes. If there are kids on the playground who do not want to play with you today, maybe you could try finding another activity to do. What could that other activity be?").

Materials

- Crayons or markers

- Paper

Directions

- Write "What's Frustrating?" across the page.

- Write down the things the child identifies as triggers for their frustration. You can also add the triggers you identify for the child.

- Put the list aside or in the child's chart for reference.

As you move through this chapter and try various calming or coping skills, come back to the list as needed. You might find that some interventions work better with one trigger than with another. The list will guide you to make sure that the child has at least one calming or coping strategy for each of their triggers.

GENERAL CALMING INTERVENTIONS

The handout on Calming Interventions is a list that provides various ideas for activities that can be calming. Look over the list with the child and discuss the following:

- How many interventions has the child tried?

- Of those tried, which ones helped them to feel calmer?

- Of those tried, which ones were not helpful?

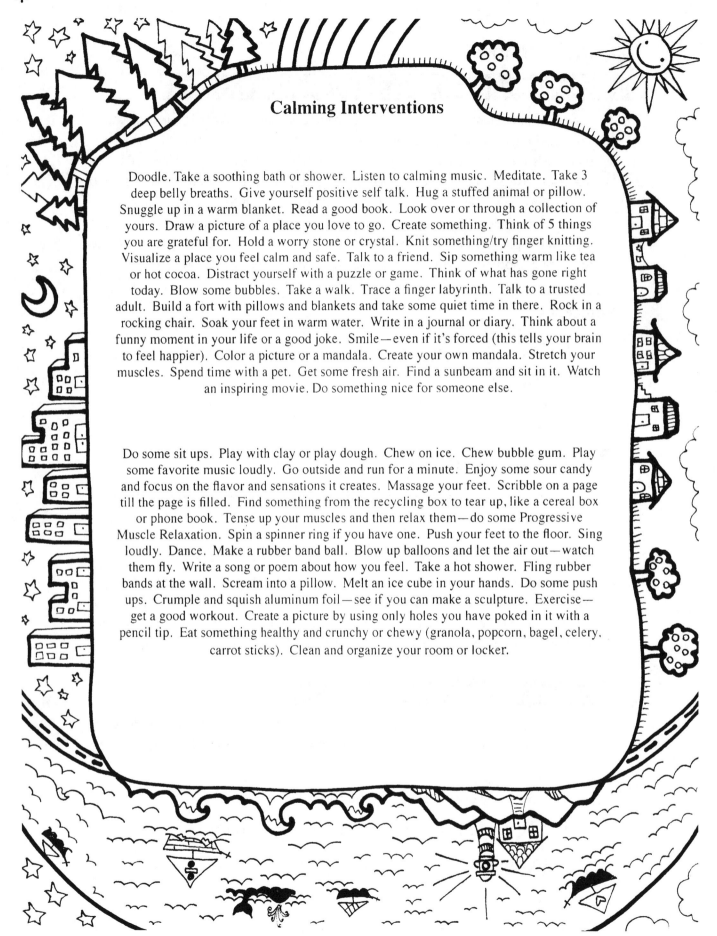

Calming Interventions

Doodle. Take a soothing bath or shower. Listen to calming music. Meditate. Take 3 deep belly breaths. Give yourself positive self talk. Hug a stuffed animal or pillow. Snuggle up in a warm blanket. Read a good book. Look over or through a collection of yours. Draw a picture of a place you love to go. Create something. Think of 5 things you are grateful for. Hold a worry stone or crystal. Knit something/try finger knitting. Visualize a place you feel calm and safe. Talk to a friend. Sip something warm like tea or hot cocoa. Distract yourself with a puzzle or game. Think of what has gone right today. Blow some bubbles. Take a walk. Trace a finger labyrinth. Talk to a trusted adult. Build a fort with pillows and blankets and take some quiet time in there. Rock in a rocking chair. Soak your feet in warm water. Write in a journal or diary. Think about a funny moment in your life or a good joke. Smile—even if it's forced (this tells your brain to feel happier). Color a picture or a mandala. Create your own mandala. Stretch your muscles. Spend time with a pet. Get some fresh air. Find a sunbeam and sit in it. Watch an inspiring movie. Do something nice for someone else.

Do some sit ups. Play with clay or play dough. Chew on ice. Chew bubble gum. Play some favorite music loudly. Go outside and run for a minute. Enjoy some sour candy and focus on the flavor and sensations it creates. Massage your feet. Scribble on a page till the page is filled. Find something from the recycling box to tear up, like a cereal box or phone book. Tense up your muscles and then relax them—do some Progressive Muscle Relaxation. Spin a spinner ring if you have one. Push your feet to the floor. Sing loudly. Dance. Make a rubber band ball. Blow up balloons and let the air out—watch them fly. Write a song or poem about how you feel. Take a hot shower. Fling rubber bands at the wall. Scream into a pillow. Melt an ice cube in your hands. Do some push ups. Crumple and squish aluminum foil—see if you can make a sculpture. Exercise—get a good workout. Create a picture by using only holes you have poked in it with a pencil tip. Eat something healthy and crunchy or chewy (granola, popcorn, bagel, celery, carrot sticks). Clean and organize your room or locker.

- Are there any interventions on this list that the child has not tried and is willing to try?

If the child can read, let them highlight the new strategies they are willing to try, or highlight the strategies they already use that work.

TRY IT, SCORE IT

Try It, Score It is a chart that helps you to keep track of the new coping and calming skills the child tries. The chart has three columns: Column 1 is for the coping and calming strategies the child is willing to try (e.g. "Tanya will take a deep breath and count to three before walking into the cafeteria.") Column 2 is for the child to score the skill (e.g. Tanya draws a smiley face in this column because this strategy helped her to feel less overwhelmed in the cafeteria). Column 3 is for the child to add a sticker. The child gets to pick out a sticker and place it in this column *even if the intervention did not work.* The sticker is earned for trying something new. If you do not have stickers, you can add a picture (e.g. draw a smiley face or heart) or a positive comment, such as: "Great job trying this one!"

The reason I love this chart is because it helps the client and I keep track of what the child has tried and what has worked. When it's time to write out an actual coping or calming plan for the child, we go to the chart and circle all the strategies that scored a smiley face.

MANAGING MY ANGER WITH RED, YELLOW, AND GREEN

Managing My Anger with Red, Yellow, and Green is a worksheet you can use to help children plan ahead for how they can recognize and manage their anger.

THE CAR TRIP

The Car Trip is a game that teaches basic anger management skills to children. The winner is the first player to complete the trip.

Materials

- The Car Trip game board sheet

- 1 die

- TUNE UP Cards, cut out from the sheet

- MAGIC WORDS Cards, cut out from the sheet

- Playing pieces (if you do not have your own playing pieces, color and make your own using the Game Pieces activity sheet)

Directions

- Youngest driver goes first.

- Roll the die and move ahead the number of spaces indicated on it.

- If you land on a TUNE UP space this means your car needs a tune up. Take a TUNE UP card and follow the directions on the card.

  [TUNE UP cards remind us that we all "break down" or need a little extra care sometimes. People are like cars in this way. When people become argumentative, hurtful, or try to make other people angry (think of a car engine that has overheated), it makes things more complicated and can make everyone involved feel frustrated. It can also delay people from getting important things done. So TUNE UP cards provide an opportunity to learn how to manage anger safely and calmly so that your "engine" is less likely to overheat or break down.]

- If you land on a TOOT YOUR HORN space, share something really awesome about yourself.

- If you land on a MAGIC WORDS space, then pick a card from that pile and answer the question on it.

  [MAGIC WORDS are words that make things easier; they are words that make people feel good; they are words that show you care for and respect other people; they are words that help you get what you need or want.]

Try it, Score it !!

☺ this helped me feel calmer ; 😐 this didn't make me feel any calmer, but it didn't make me feel worse ; ☹ this made me feel worse

This is the new calming or coping skill that I tried:	This is how I scored it :	A sticker or picture or comment for trying it :

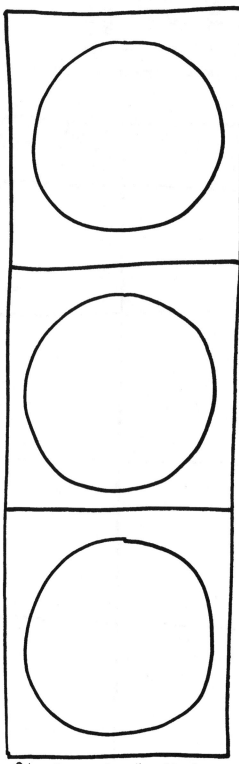

MANAGING MY ANGER USING RED, YELLOW, AND GREEN

RED: When I'm feeling "RED" it means I feel really angry! These are the things I can do to calm myself down and stay safe:

_____
_____
_____
_____

YELLOW: When I'm feeling "YELLOW" it means I'm starting to feel annoyed or agitated. This is the perfect time to try these things to feel calmer:

_____
_____
_____
_____

GREEN: When I'm feeling "GREEN" it means I feel calm and/or happy.

Color the circles the same color that is written next to them.

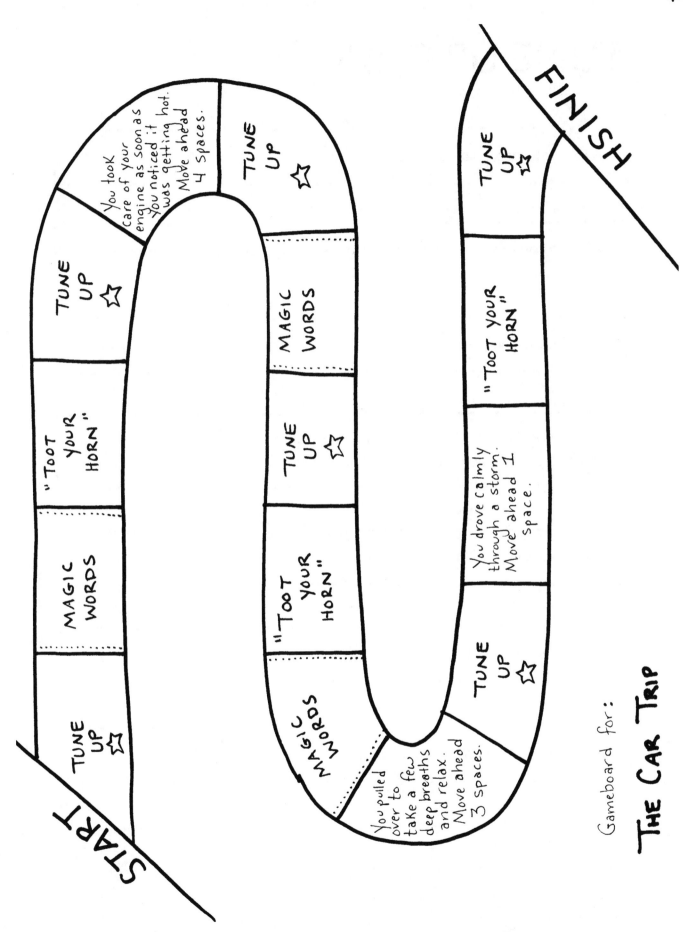

START

FINISH

TUNE UP ☆

"TOOT YOUR HORN"

MAGIC WORDS

TUNE UP ☆

You took care of your engine as soon as you noticed it was getting hot. Move ahead 4 spaces.

TUNE UP ☆

MAGIC WORDS

TUNE UP ☆

"TOOT YOUR HORN"

MAGIC WORDS

You pulled over to take a few deep breaths and relax. Move ahead 3 spaces.

TUNE UP ☆

You drove calmly through a storm. Move ahead 1 space.

"TOOT YOUR HORN"

TUNE UP ☆

Gameboard for:

The Car Trip

COPYRIGHT © BONNIE THOMAS 2016

TUNE UP Cards

Take three deep, relaxing breaths.

Why do you think some kids make other kids angry and upset on purpose?

Think about, and then describe, something that has gone right for you today.

Stand up and stretch. Sometimes when we feel stressed out or upset, stretching can be a gentle way to take a quick break to calm our bodies down.

Name one safe way to release anger.

How do some people show they are angry?

Squeeze all the muscles in your hands, legs and arms. Then relax them. Sometimes when you are angry this can be a safe and quick way to release some anger.

Does everybody have bad days now and then? Of course they do! The next time you are having a bad day, remind yourself that bad days happen to everybody, not just you. You are not alone. We all know how horrible a bad day can feel.

Count backwards, slowly, from 10 to 1.

Tell the other players about something funny you have seen, heard, or experienced. Humor can sometimes help people feel more relaxed. Laughing relieves stress.

Tell the other players about a way you like to relax.

Tell the other players about a place that feels safe and relaxing to you.

Tell the players about someone you know who always seems to be calm or relaxed.

Some people feel calmer when they see pictures or videos of baby animals. Tell the other players about one of your favorite baby animals. Do you love puppies? Kittens? Other baby animals?

MAGIC WORDS Cards

Which one of these phrases has MAGIC WORDS in them:

☐ No way!

☐ Yes, please.

☐ Go away.

Which one of these sentences has MAGIC WORDS in them:

☐ I wanted something else!

☐ That's not fair!

☐ Thank you.

Which of these responses uses MAGIC WORDS?

☐ I'm not going to do that!

☐ Do it yourself!

☐ Sure! I'll do my best.

Which one of these phrases has MAGIC WORDS in it?

☐ My spoon is purple.

☐ Please and thank you.

☐ Kangaroos hop.

Find the phrase that has the MAGIC WORDS in it:

☐ Please hand me that pencil.

☐ Give me that pencil!

☐ Give me that pencil, NOW!

*

·······Game Pieces··········

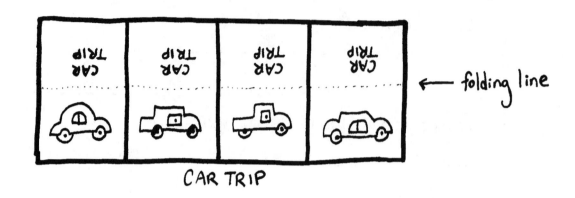

CAR TRIP

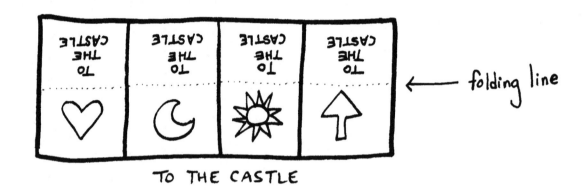

TO THE CASTLE

Cut the four playing pieces out for the game you're playing. Cut on the BOLD lines. FOLD on the ······ dotted lines.

Skill: Breathing

It sounds silly to say that breathing is a skill, because we do it unconsciously. However, many people tend to hold their breath or breathe into their ribcage when they are feeling frustration and stress. There's a more effective way to breathe to help manage anger and other strong emotions—like anxiety—by breathing into your stomach. It's called "belly breathing." Another breathing strategy is to exhale with a forceful breath (not all the time, just in a moment of tension).

The following activities provide ways for children to practice various breathing techniques to help them get their breath moving. As with any exercise involving breathing, if you or the child starts to feel faint or light-headed, stop the activity.

Interventions

KEEP THE FEATHER IN THE AIR

Give the child a small feather and see how long they can keep it afloat by blowing it into the air. This activity encourages the child to exhale with focused and forceful breath, releasing tension.

BLOWING BALLOONS

Have the child blow up a balloon and then let go of it (do not tie the neck of the balloon). Not only does this exercise provide a fun way to practice inhaling and exhaling, it's also funny when the balloon flies all over the place once you let go of it. Laughing is another way to relieve tension, so if this activity brings a good laugh to the child, all the better.

Allergy note: Make sure the child is not allergic to latex if doing this activity. Many balloons are made of latex.

BREATHE FIRE LIKE A DRAGON

Younger children can practice forceful exhaling with this age-appropriate activity of breathing out like a dragon. The child holds the paper tube up to his mouth (the tube is created to look like a dragon's snout) and then breathes out forcefully to "see" the tissue paper flames moving.

Materials

- Scissors

- Red, yellow, and orange tissue paper

- Paper tube for the dragon's snout (you can make your own tube out of rolled paper or use a toilet paper tube or other cardboard tube)

- Glue stick

- Markers

- Pompoms and googly eyes (optional)

Directions

- Cut the tissue paper into thin strips or shaped like flames, about 5–10 in (13–25 cm), depending on the length of the dragon's snout.

- Glue the ends of the tissue paper flames to the inside rim of the tube. Allow the glue to dry.

- Use markers to color the tube green or some other dragon color. Use a dark marker to draw scales over the skin color.

- Create nostrils and eyes on the dragon's snout if you like. To do this, first roll tissue paper into small balls to make nostrils, then glue them on the end of the snout; next, make mini tubes from small strips of paper and glue those on for eyes or nostrils; alternatively, attach pompoms and googly eyes with glue.

- Allow the glue to dry.

- Blow through the tube and watch the "flames" move!

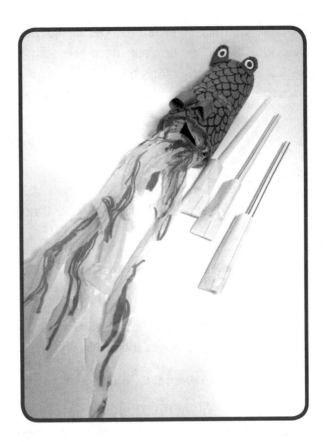

LAVA STRAWS

This activity is especially useful for children who are visual learners and/or have difficulty expressing their feelings verbally.

Volcanoes are a wonderful metaphor for anger. Some people have "volcanoes" that are explosive and dangerous. Others might have a "volcano" that bubbles up and spits lava here and there, but mostly stays under control. And some people even have a quiet or dormant "volcano" that never seems to erupt at all.

Talk to the child about their anger: If their anger were a volcano, what kind of volcano would they have? What kind of volcano would their mom or dad have? Or their sister? Whose volcano erupts the most? The loudest? Are there any family members who have a dormant volcano? Whose volcano causes the most damage? You can discuss these questions while you make these Lava Straws.

You can use Lava Straws a couple of ways with kids:

- Use Lava Straws to create messy lava patterns—the child gets the practice of deep breathing and strong, controlled exhales.

- Use Lava Straws as a metaphor and a visual for how explosive anger can be. Ask the child to create and compare lava from volcanoes belonging to family or friends. For example: "When your sister gets angry, what does the lava from her volcano look like?" "When you get angry, what does the lava from your volcano look like?" "When your mom gets angry, what does the lava from her volcano look like?" When the child has made a few lava pictures, you can discuss how they differ or how they are the same.

Materials

- Large sheet/s of paper

- Yellow, orange, and red tempera paint (add water if needed)

- Straws

Directions

- Put a large sheet of paper on a flat surface. Remove or cover any items in the surrounding area that could get splattered with paint.

- Place a small pile of paint where the "volcano" is.

- Give the child a straw. Explain that they can blow air OUT of the straw to move the paint around the paper. Let the child experiment with various strengths of breath so they can see which breath makes splatters and explosions vs. little movement at all.

STRAW ROCKETS

Straw Rockets are a fun, simple way to get kids moving their breath and releasing tension. Provide targets for the child to aim at such as a poster on the wall or into a basket.

Caution: Straw Rockets can be aimed and fired, so go over safety guidelines and common sense rules as necessary with the child. For example, a common sense rule is "Do not aim Straw Rockets at people." If the child is prone to use these carelessly (e.g. they have siblings and it's just too tempting to take a shot), then move on to another activity.

Materials

- Lightweight paper (e.g. notebook paper)

- Tape and scissors

- Plastic straws

Directions

- Cut small rectangles out of recycled paper, about 3 x 1 in (7.5 x 2.5 cm).

- Fold one of the paper rectangles in half, lengthwise.

- Place tape along the long edge of the rectangle where the paper edges meet.

- Next, fold the top edge of the rectangle over and then tape that into place.

- After all of these steps you should now have a mini-pocket for the straw to fit into.

- Insert a straw into the "rocket." Leave a little room at the end of the rocket for air to reach it (do not push the straw all the way to the tip of the rocket).

- Finally, blow through the straw and the rocket should fly!

FREEZE! BREATHE!

Freeze! Breathe! is a quick game you can play with one or more kids in an open space. The rules of the game are simple—go about your normal activity but at various times you can say "Freeze! Breathe!" The child then has to freeze on the spot and take three deep breaths before going back to the activity. Some kids love this game because it's spontaneous and a bit silly. The benefit of playing it is to teach the child impulse control skills (Freeze!) in addition to mindful breathing (Breathe!).

 ## Skill: Using sensory input to release frustration

The following activities provide stress relief specifically for those children who benefit from added sensory input when they are angry. These are the kids who love squeezing stress balls, punching pillows, or screaming when they are upset.

 ## Interventions

BUBBLE WRAP DISPENSERS

Materials

- A recycled tissue box (the kind that has an opening in the box for dispensing tissues)

- Scissors

- Scrap pieces of recycled bubble wrap

- Materials for decoration—paint, decorative paper, etc. (optional)

Directions

- If you like, decorate the outside of the tissue box. You could paint the box, cover it in decorative paper, or decoupage it.

- Cut scraps of bubble wrap into squares or rectangles to fit inside the tissue box.

- Whenever the child is showing signs of frustration, remind them to take a "sheet" of bubble wrap and pop the bubbles.

ALUMINUM FOIL SCULPTURES

Aluminum foil has a texture that allows a child to shape it and squish it. Provide some aluminum foil and encourage the child to shape it and squeeze it into balls or create a sculpture. The squeezing will help release tension in the hands and body.

PENCIL POINT PICTURES

A Pencil Point Picture is made by pushing a pencil tip into areas of a picture to create texture (in this case the texture is polka dots). This drawing activity provides some sensory input and muscle pressure, which can help to release tension and frustration.

Materials

- A sharpened pencil

- Plain paper

- A thick piece of cardboard

Directions

- Draw a picture on one side of the paper, making sure that one area will be decorated with multiple dots—the dots could be snow or rain, sand on a beach, whiskers on a person's face (perfect for drawing pirates), a rash on someone's skin, or just filling in negative space.

- Darken the lines surrounding where the dots are, or darken the dots themselves. You will want to be able to see them from the other side of the paper when you flip it over.

- Flip the picture over and place it on the cardboard.

- Press your pencil tip into each dot and/or fill any darkened areas with dots.

- When all the dots and/or darkened areas have been pressed with your pencil tip, flip the picture back over. The areas you dotted will now have a texture to them.

COTTON BALL SLAM

This is a silly, but helpful, activity for releasing frustration, which works best with kids who have a goofy sense of humor. Keep a small basket or container of cotton balls in the home or office. When your child or client becomes upset, give them the option to have a Cotton Ball Slam—they get to "slam" each cotton ball to the ground as hard as they can. Of course, no matter how hard you throw a cotton ball, it's not going to slam. But some kids have fun trying, and release a lot of built-up tension in the process. I've seen kids go through an entire basket of cotton balls, alone and with friends, and it usually results in stress release as a result of the physical activity and laughter.

STRESS BALLS

Stress balls can be purchased in many styles, but it's helpful to know how to make your own in case you need a quantity of them or want to make them as a group activity. Stress balls are great to have for those kids who benefit from squeezing something or releasing tension when they are upset.

Materials

Allergy note: This activity uses balloons and play dough, both of which contain allergens (balloons have latex, and play dough has wheat/gluten). Make sure the child is not allergic to these items before doing this activity.

- Play dough

- Balloons—a bag of good quality balloons (the stronger, the better)

Directions

- Provide the child with a handful of play dough and give them a few moments to play with it if necessary.

- Ask the child to form the play dough into several small balls, about the size of a raisin.

- Hold the neck of a balloon open—you will need both hands for this, and you will need to stretch the neck of the balloon as wide as it allows without breaking.

- Have the child put their play dough balls into the balloon through the neck.

- If necessary, add additional play dough. You want the equivalent of a small handful of play dough in the balloon.

- Tie the neck of the balloon.

- Now the child has their own stress ball! They can squish it and squeeze it if feeling angry or needing some sensory input.

- Discuss how and when the child might use the stress ball as a calming strategy.

 # Skill: Taking a break

The following activities encourage children to take a break when they need to calm their mind and bodies.

✚ Interventions

. . . .

SNOW GLOBE

If a child is angry or frustrated, they might like a Snow Globe added to their collection of calming "tools." This can be satisfying to shake up if they're feeling angry. Children, in general, find Snow Globes fun because they are interactive and it's soothing to watch the snow settle. Some parents even use Snow Globes with "time outs" by having the child shake them up and take deep breaths while the "snow" falls to the bottom. When the snow has settled, the time out is over—this is especially helpful for children who respond well to visual cues.

Materials

- Jar with a lid (you can use recycled jars from food products, but make sure they have been cleaned and that the labels and label adhesives have been removed)

- Small plastic cap from a soda bottle (if making a small snow globe), or a plastic cap from a vitamin or medicine bottle (if making a larger snow globe)

- Industrial strength glue that adheres to metal, plastic, and glass (e.g. E6000)

- Plastic figurine

- Water

- Glitter

- Glycerin

Directions

- Place the jar lid on a flat surface. The lid becomes the base of the snow globe, so make sure the lid is facing upward where you can see the inside rim.

- Add your plastic bottle cap to the inside of the lid. Apply the glue to the rim of the cap and then glue it into the center of the jar lid. You want the smooth and flat surface of the cap to be facing upward because this is where you will glue the figurine.

- Glue the figurine to the center of the cap.

- Allow the glue to dry and cure, as stated on the directions.

- Make sure the jar you are using is clean. Fill the jar almost to the top with water.

- Add glitter—add a little at a time until you like the consistency.

- Add a few drops of glycerin.

- Screw the lid onto the jar. Make sure it is screwed on tightly.

- Flip the jar over and apply more of the industrial strength glue all around the seal of the lid.

- Allow the glue to dry.

- Your Snow Globe is now done—shake it up and give it a try!

GLITTER BOTTLE

A Glitter Bottle is like a Snow Globe without the figurine inside. It works well with children who get upset quickly. The glitter in the bottle is a lot like our feelings—when we get "shaken up," we can feel like our thoughts and feelings are all over the place. But if we quiet our bodies and minds by breathing and tuning into the moment, the glitter will start to settle to the bottom of the bottle, much like feelings do when they calm down. The Glitter Bottle is a simple demonstration for showing how feelings are temporary and they settle down. If we quiet our breathing, and tune into the moment, we can observe the feeling in our bodies and mind and wait for it to pass—much like glitter drifting slowly down to the bottom of the bottle.

Materials

- A clear plastic soda bottle

- Water

- Glitter (you can combine one or more types of glitter)

- Glycerin

Directions

- Wash the plastic bottle and make sure the label and its adhesives have been removed.

- Fill the bottle almost to the top with water—leave room for glitter.

- Add the glitter. Add a little at a time until you like the consistency and amount of glitter.

- Add a few drops of glycerin to the water and glitter.

- Put the bottle cap on and secure it tightly.

- Shake the contents of the bottle to allow the glitter, glycerin, and water to mix.

SAFETY ZONES AND MEDITATION STATIONS

A Safety Zone is an area where the child knows they can go to calm down. A Meditation Station is similar in that it's a place for the child to go to calm down and/ or meditate. Whichever you call it, it's a safe spot where the child can go when they feel overwhelmed. The space might have a stuffed animal, "fidgets" (see page 58), a Glitter Bottle, or other items that help them to self-soothe and calm down. Here are some examples of ways to create Safety Zones or Meditation Stations in your own home or office:

- Make or purchase a small kid-sized teepee. (I use one of these in my office for a quiet space when kids need it.)

- Use tape or paint to mark off a corner or area in a room where the child can set up their Safety Zone on their own—children often love to design and set up their own spaces.

- Remove the door from a small closet and allow the child to set up a space inside.

- Build a blanket and pillow fort for temporary space. You can also put a large blanket over a table or desk for an on-the-spot area.

- Decorate a large cardboard box and cut out a door and windows.

 ## An accompanying story

The Robot's Fuse

Fizz was a young robot who loved to go to the playground. His favorite part of the playground was going on the swing set, but many times he had to wait a long time for his turn on the swing. Sometimes Fizz was patient while he waited for his turn, and sometimes he was not.

One day, Fizz was waiting for his turn on the swing. And waiting. And waiting. Fizz had been waiting a long time but none of the other robots were getting off the swings. Fizz started to feel impatient and angry. The more he thought about waiting, the angrier he got. And angrier. And ANGRIER. He could feel his bolts getting hot. He could feel tension in the wires across his chest. The rivets on his head were getting tighter and tighter.

Then all of a sudden, Fizz blew a fuse. He completely malfunctioned! Steam started coming out of his ears. The antennae on his head turned bright red. And then Fizz started shouting and throwing his arms about. There was a loud BOOM! SIZZLE! CRACK! And then Fizz shut down.

Later that afternoon Fizz and his mom had a talk about what happened. Fizz's mom said she was upset that she had to leave her job to come get Fizz—she needed to work and she was also embarrassed he had acted this way. She wondered what happened—she wondered how Fizz became THAT angry...SO angry...that he actually blew a fuse!

After Fizz described what happened at the playground, his mom helped him recognize some moments when he could have listened to his thoughts and body for clues that he was getting angry. She also went over some things he could do next time to help calm those thoughts and his body so that he doesn't blow a fuse. She said it might take practice, but if he listened to her advice, he would get better at keeping his fuse from blowing.

The next day, Fizz went to the playground. Sure enough, there was a line for the swings. "Oh great—there's a line. AGAIN. Why is there always a line?" Fizz thought to himself.

Fizz noticed right away that this thought was negative. His mom told him yesterday that negative thoughts can make you feel angry. She told him that if negative thoughts came into his head, he could change them to positive ones. Changing his thoughts into positive ones would help him feel less frustrated about the situation. So Fizz thought for a moment and then said to himself: "Looks like there is a line today—I guess I can take some deep breaths and watch the other kids swing for a moment. Or I can look at the sky for fun cloud shapes. Or I can see if there are any beautiful flowers or insects in the grass. Or I can talk to the robot next to me in line."

Fizz noticed that instead of getting angry, he was feeling a little calmer. He still wanted his turn on the swing, but whenever he thought about feeling impatient, he would think about something positive instead. He would also take a deep cleansing breath. These things did help him feel like he could wait a minute longer if needed.

When it was Fizz's turn on the swing, he was proud of himself for staying calm and not blowing a fuse. By not blowing a fuse, he got to do and finish the things he wanted to.

The more that Fizz practiced this, the easier it got for him to notice when his thoughts were turning negative, and the easier it got for him to turn those negative thoughts into positive ones. From that day forward Fizz knew that as soon as negative thoughts came into his head, he needed to quiet them by thinking about what was going right and okay.

An activity to go along with the story

MAKE A ROBOT

These robots made from recyclable materials are a fun and creative activity for kids!

Materials

- 2 recycled boxes (one box will be the robot's head and the other will be the robot's body—boxes from cereals, crackers, cookies, over-the-counter medicines, and bandages work well)

- Recycled paper

- Clear tape

- Aluminum foil

- Glue gun and glue

- Various metal objects: paperclips, small hardware (i.e. washers, small screws, blown fuses), discarded metal jewelry parts, etc.

Directions

- Stuff the boxes with recycled paper. Then tape the box lids shut.

- Wrap each box in aluminum foil as if you were wrapping a present. Aluminum foil tears easily, so repair or re-wrap places as necessary.

- Smooth any bumps or ridges of the foil and then tape the foil down in place.

- Use hot glue to attach the boxes to each other—one box is the head and the other is the body.

- Have the child pick out metal pieces to create the robot's face.

- Use the glue gun to glue the metal parts to the robot's face.

- Have the child pick out the pieces of metal to decorate the robot's body. Glue these on with the hot glue as well.

- Create arms and legs for the robot by rolling aluminum foil into leg and arm shapes.

- Attach the arms and legs using the hot glue gun. Arms can be glued to the sides of the body. Legs can be attached to the bottom of the body. You can also glue the top of the legs to the bottom of the robot's back and then along the bottom of the body if you want the robot to be able to sit (e.g. on a shelf).

- Repair any areas if necessary. Add hot glue to any areas that need extra stabilization.

- Remind the child that the robot can break easily—if the child wants to keep the robot for a long time they can ask the adult at home to put it up on a shelf or away for safe-keeping. The adult can also take a photo of the robot to preserve the memory of it.

 Affirmations

✓ I can calm my body.

✓ I am in control of my body.

✓ Deep breaths.

CHAPTER 5

Increasing Focus and Reducing Impulsivity

! Challenge

The child is impulsive, distractible, inattentive, unfocused, "on the go, all the time."

◎ Goals

The child will be able to stop and think before acting.

The child will be able to sustain attention and focus when needed.

The child will stretch their attention span so that they are able to focus on an activity for _____ minutes.

⚙ Skills: Impulse reduction and increased focus

In a fast paced culture, it can feel like an uphill battle teaching children to slow down, observe their surroundings, and apply thought-out plans as opposed to just acting and reacting. The following activities encourage children to increase their focus and attention, to remember details and apply information they have learned, to reduce impulsivity, and to stop and think before acting.

➕ Interventions

MEMORY

Memory is a card game that encourages players to use and strengthen their memory and attention skills. In this game you have several pairs of cards that feature the same image. For example, two cards might have images of a flower and another two cards might have images of a forest, and so forth until you have several pairs of matching images. The cards are shuffled and placed face down so that you can't see any of the pictures. Player 1 turns over two cards in the hope of finding a matching pair. If no match is found, the player places the cards face down (where they took them from) and then it is Player 2's turn. As the game progresses, each player tries to remember where they have seen the images in order to create matches. When a player does find a match, they can take an extra turn. The game ends when all the matches have been made. The winner is the person who has found the most matches.

Memory games can be purchased if you prefer. However, you can also use a regular deck of cards by splitting the deck into pairs of matching numbers. For younger kids or children with short attention spans, start with a smaller number of matches (e.g. five matches) and then work your way up to a larger number.

RED LIGHT, GREEN LIGHT

Red Light, Green Light is a popular game among young children, which can be modified for groups or an individual. It helps children to be more aware of their ability to stop, and be in control of, their bodies.

To play as a group, children form a line along a "starting line." There is one caller for the game—the caller stays at the finish line and calls out "red light" or "green light." If the caller says "green light!" then all the kids move quickly toward the "finish line." If the caller says "red light!" then the players must freeze in place. The caller makes a quick observation of the "frozen" players. If any of the players move, they have to go back to the "starting line." The caller then continues to call out "red light!" and "green light!" at intervals of their choosing. The first player who reaches the "finish line!" is the winner.

If you are with only one child you can modify the game. As a clinician I have played the game with clients going to and from my office. If I call out "red light!" and the child moves, we might go back to the starting point (e.g. the waiting room). You can keep track of how long it takes you to get to your office each session and then try to break those "records."

You can also play a generalized version of the game where you call out "red light!" and "green light!" on walks, at the park, at the beach, or even in the house. Some kids enjoy the simple challenge of "freezing" in place.

MAKING MARBLE TRACKS

Children are usually fascinated by building tracks that marbles can follow. But building a successful marble track takes patience, focus, and determination, which can be especially challenging for children with impulsive behaviors or difficulty with attention. One way that I use marble tracks in my counseling practice is to tell the client we will build marble tracks twice.

The first time we build the track, we will dive right in and just build—no planning, no discussion, no looking at the directions for how the pieces connect. We set the timer for 20 minutes and see what we can accomplish.

For the second trial, we make a plan before building. We discuss what might be helpful for us to know before we build (e.g. do we need to look at directions? Should we agree on who is working on the beginning of the track and who is constructing the finish?). Then we set the timer for 20 minutes and see what we can accomplish.

Finally, we have a follow-up discussion about how the first trial and second differed (if they did). Many times the child will be able to differentiate between the trials and recognize the pros and cons of diving in vs. planning ahead. You can use the following discussion questions:

- Did you get more creative results with one trial vs. the other?

- Did either trial end up with a completed track?

- Which track was your favorite and why?

- Which track was harder to build? Why?

If you work with children, then you may prefer to purchase a marble track because the purchased sets are more durable and easier to store. But if you are the care provider or parent for the child, you can collect recyclables and design your own Marble Track. Cardboard tubes, foam trays, and small boxes can be taped together to create your own custom version.

BUILDING WITH BLOCKS

Building blocks activities usually require the child to use "stop and think" skills. Although many children go through a phase of knocking blocks over, this phase does pass and the child matures enough actually to want to construct something. Whether the child is building with wood blocks, plastic interlocking blocks, or another block design, building will require some thought and patience. Allow the child to experiment with various building block sets to see if there is a style that appeals to them. Some block sets come with instructions for building a certain item; other sets encourage more "free style" creating. Either way, your child will benefit from block play. If the child has trouble thinking of things to create, you can always create a "Build it" Jar (see below).

THE "BUILD IT" JAR

Materials

- Scissors

- Paper

- Pen

- A medium size jar with lid (cleaned and dried)

Directions

- Cut the paper into strips. Write the following suggestions on separate strips of paper:

  » house
  » barn
  » chicken coop
  » cave
  » car garage
  » hideout
  » bridge
  » tunnel
  » alien ship
  » pirate ship
  » spaceship
  » van
  » camper
  » hot rod vehicle
  » construction vehicle
  » speedboat
  » jet skis
  » airplane
  » robots

  » people
  » animals
  » moon landscape
  » city
  » castle
  » maze
  » spell something out
  » build a scene from a favorite book or movie
  » secret compartment
  » mailbox
  » race car
  » monster truck
  » jail
  » obstacle course for a figurine
  » bakery
  » city park
  » marina

- » coal mine
- » fenced-in areas for animal figurines
- » track and field course
- » space station
- » time machine
- » food items

- » superhero base/ supervillain lair
- » theater
- » dungeon
- » crystal cave
- » mermaid's pool

- Fold each strip in half and put them all in the jar.

- When your child is not sure what to build or create with blocks, he or she can pull out an idea and try it.

SCAVENGER HUNT

The Scavenger Hunt encourages the use of focus, attention, and sometimes even memory skills. Children are given a list of items to find. The list of items will depend on the location of the hunt. If any of the players are not reading yet, the list can be made with pictures rather than words.

Scavenger Hunt list ideas

At the grocery store

Note: Make sure the children are checking off the items and NOT putting them in your cart. They can write the aisle number they found the item in or describe where they found it in place of actually gathering the items.

Simple: Something that grew on a tree; something square shaped; something that has a picture of a cow on it; something blue; something soft; something with the number 5 on it.

Challenging: Something in a red box; a fruit from Central America; something that has Madagascar vanilla in the ingredients; something that costs exactly _____; something carbonated that does not have caffeine; something over 400 calories per serving; something that made you smile; a candy that does not have any food dyes in it; a coupon someone left behind in the aisle.

On a nature walk

Simple: A rock; a leaf; something green; something smaller than your thumbnail; something rough; something smooth; a twig that is shaped like a Y; an acorn cap; a pine cone; a bottle cap.

Challenging: Leaves in three different colors or three different shades of one color; a collection of twigs that can spell out "YAY!"; a flower that smells good; a stick figure made from natural materials found on your walk; a feather; a strange formation in a tree; a cloud that looks like an object or animal; a strange footprint; something you'd find in a fantasy book; a seed.

In the home

Simple: Something soft; something that you can write with; something in the shape of a rectangle; something cold; something shiny; an eating utensil; something that starts with the letter S; a book; a remote; something green; a hat.

Challenging: A price tag; five paperclips; something that broke off of an object; a sock that doesn't have a match; spare change; lint formed into the shape of any animal; something that smells sour; something that starts with the letter J; something you could wrap or decorate a gift with; something that makes a noise; something curly; an empty can.

At school

Simple: A ruler; a pencil; something that starts with the letter W; a book with a long title; a book with a short title; a sticker; something with stripes; a map; the principal's autograph; a pink eraser.

Challenging: An equation; a compound word; a calculator; an empty trash can; a book published before 2000; something written in cursive; a stick figure of a person drawn and signed by a teacher; a book written by an author whose name starts with the letter A; erasers in three different colors; something geometric.

I SPY

I Spy is a game that encourages children to observe their surroundings and practice mindfulness.

To play, one player looks around and finds something they "spy" that the other players will try to guess. The player says, "I spy with my eye something that…" and they will name an object that starts with a certain letter, is a certain color, or has a certain pattern. For example, if the player chooses a stop sign for their object, they could say "I spy with my eye something that starts with the letter S," or they could say "I spy with my eye something that is red." The other player/s take turns guessing what it could be until someone figures out the object. The person who guesses correctly takes the next turn.

HUCKLEBERRY BEANSTALK

Huckleberry Beanstalk is a game that I played in my elementary school when I was little. The game is also referred to as Huckle Buckle Beanstalk. I probably loved the name more than anything else but I have fond memories of playing this game with my peers. I now play the game with my clients because it's another game that teaches observation and mindfulness skills.

To play, choose a small object that can be easily identified and is the only one of its kind in the room. I have used everything from a spool of red thread to a fun figurine to an eraser. You can play Huckleberry Beanstalk with any number of players.

Have the child cover their eyes or step out of the room (do not leave young or unsafe children unattended). Hide the object in the room where the child will be able to see it. There is no hands on in this game so the object must be hidden in a place where eyes can find it without having to move or touch anything.

Now have the child uncover their eyes or return to the room. Their job is to try to find the object without touching anything. When the child does find the object, they say "Huckleberry Beanstalk!" If you are playing this in a group, the child says "Huckleberry Beanstalk!" and then sits down and waits for everyone else to find the object.

SPINNING TOPS

Spinning Tops can be an engaging activity for children who are curious and enjoy sensory stimulation. The added bonus of playing with more than one top at a time is that it takes a level of focus and attention in order to keep them going. I find this activity helps to develop some attention skills as well as multitasking.

Directions

Let the child explore a variety of tops. They can practice spinning each top to get a feel for how each one feels (some spin faster, some are weighted and feel heavier, some are harder to balance than others, etc.). Once the child has a sense for how they work and feel, let them experiment with how many tops they can keep spinning at once. There is no right or wrong here—just allow the child to explore and play with the tops.

JUMPING BEANS

Now and then I purchase "jumping beans" for my office. What I love about jumping beans is that you can warm them in your hands and then put them on a flat surface to watch them "jump." But they only "jump" after they've been left alone for a few minutes. If you get impatient and poke or jostle the beans, they will remain or become quiet. Children want to see the beans move, so they have to keep their hands to themselves and wait. This is good practice in impulse control.

FINGER LABYRINTH

A labyrinth is an ancient design created by circuitous winding paths, which can be used for meditation and mindfulness practice. There are several types of labyrinth, both in design and in form. For the purpose of this book I will focus on the Finger Labyrinth, in which you use your finger to follow the path of the labyrinth. For children who are working on slowing their minds and bodies, the Finger Labyrinth can be a way of practicing focus and concentration as well as relaxation.

Here are instructions for how you can make your own Finger Labyrinth (this is simple enough to do with children). Children tend to enjoy the tactile feel of this particular labyrinth.

Materials

- Scissors

- Printout of the three-circuit Finger Labyrinth template

- Paper plate

- Regular glue stick

- Glue gun and glue

- Aluminum foil

Directions

- Cut a circle around the labyrinth. Glue the labyrinth to the center of the paper plate using the glue stick (not the hot glue).

- Plug in the glue gun. Apply hot glue along the black line of the labyrinth— this is the boundary of the labyrinth.

- Allow the hot glue to harden. Remove any excess glue strings.

- Repeat the above step one or two more times as necessary. The thicker and higher the labyrinth boundary is, the easier the finger labyrinth will be to use.

- Tear off a sheet of aluminum foil. Apply glue from the glue stick to one side of the aluminum foil. Then press the aluminum foil onto the paper plate.

- Gently press the aluminum foil into place around the hardened hot glue areas. Fold excess aluminum foil around the edges of the plate.

- Add aluminum foil as necessary until the entire plate is covered and smoothed down. By now the labyrinth should be visible and there should be a small grooved path for your finger to follow.

- Allow the glue to dry.

- Now the child can use their finger to follow the pathway into the center of the labyrinth and back out again.

ALTERNATIVE FINGER LABYRINTH

This version of a Finger Labyrinth works better for older kids and adults because it is more durable but costs more for the supplies.

Materials

- Glue

- Printout of the three-circuit Finger Labyrinth template

- Flat piece of wood or thick cardboard, about 12 x 12 in (30 x 30 cm) (suggestion: if you have an old vinyl record in its cover that is no longer usable, recycle it for this project!)

- Twine, thin cord, or thick string

- Paint

Directions

- Glue the template for the finger labyrinth to the surface of the wood or cardboard. Allow it to dry.

- Apply glue to the lines of the labyrinth.

- Place the twine or cord on the glued lines—you may need to put a heavy object on top to hold it in place where it curves.

- Allow the twine and glue to dry. Check on it a few times to make sure everything stays in place while drying.

- Paint over the entire surface, including the labyrinth. Allow the paint to dry.

- Add additional layers of paint as needed and allow the paint to dry.

- Add pictures, designs, or patterns around the labyrinth if you like.

Template for making a
"Finger Labyrinth"

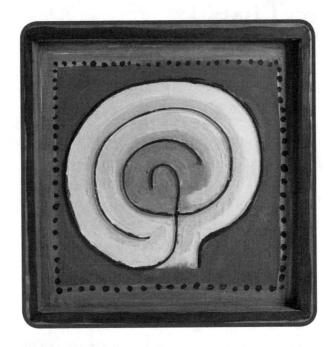

STORE-BOUGHT GAMES

There are many commercial games that encourage players to slow down and focus in order to have an advantage to winning the game. These games include (but are not limited to) Jenga®, Operation®, Honey Bee Tree®, Sperlunk®, Potzblitz®, Memory®, Don't Break the Ice®, Connect 4®, Don't Spill the Beans®, Monkeying Around®, and Pick Up Sticks®. Jigsaw puzzles are also wonderful interventions to develop these skills.

Use these games and puzzles on a regular basis to help your children or clients practice focusing skills, impulse control, and attention skills.

FOCUSING TIPS

The following handout has a list of suggestions that can help reduce distractions for those needing to focus on a task at hand, i.e. studying or writing a school paper. Sometimes older clients keep a handout in their academic planner or even taped to their desk at home where they do most of their school work. The handout provides a concrete reference for the older child to refer to as needed.

*

Focusing Tips

- Utilize apps on your smartphone that provide games to train your brain with skills like focusing and multitasking (e.g. Lumosity®, CogniFit® and NeuroNation®).

- Also, take advantage of apps on your smartphone that help with organization, such as calendars, notes, and lists.

- Keep a regular schedule or routine, especially with sleep. It's harder to focus when you are exhausted.

- Use an appointment book or assignment book to keep track of tasks, assignments, and appointments that need to be done. Keep it with you!

- Break larger projects/assignments down into smaller ones. Use your appointment or assignment book to set deadlines for completing each stage of the project.

- If you have a hard time sitting still, try using a "fidget" to see if that helps you sit still for longer. For example, have an adult sew a piece of Velcro into the inside of your pocket. Velcro has a texture that is fun to fidget with! Or find a small item to keep in your pocket that you can fidget with (e.g. a bottle cap, an elastic band, a paper clip, something fuzzy, a piece of corduroy, or a small stress ball).

- When working on a project that takes focus (e.g. a school paper), try the following routine:

  - Clear your work space of all distractions. This includes shutting off your phone or devices that are not needed to complete your task.

  - Turn on some white noise or a fan. This will block out other distracting noises.

  - Make a list of what you need to get done during this time.

  - Set a timer if you need to. A timer can remind you to move on to the next phase of your "to do" list.

- If you have access to one, use a yoga ball or a balance disc to sit on while you work.

- Take breaks to stretch or walk around the room if you start to feel unfocused.

- If reading, highlight key phrases or take written notes of what you have read.

- If you get distracted by your own thoughts (e.g. "I forgot to tell the coach that I won't be at practice on Wednesday" or "I wonder if I have enough money to buy that new game?"), then write these thoughts and questions down on a separate piece of paper. You can go back to those things later—for now you need to stay focused on the task at hand.

- Keep a snack and some water at hand. Some people focus better when they have a piece of spicy or minty candy, something crunchy or chewy, or something sour to eat. Chewing gum can also help.

- Sometimes "fidgets" can be helpful (unless they make you even more distracted). If they are helpful to you, keep one or two fidgets at your work space.

- If you have more suggestions, write them here:

_____

_____

_____

_____

_____

_____

_____

_____

_____

_____

_____

An accompanying story
The Pirate Who Lost His Treasure

A long, long time ago there was a pirate who was getting ready to retire from his life at sea and he needed to complete one very important task before he could settle down and leave his pirate life behind. He had to find the treasure he had buried long ago. When he was a younger pirate, he had buried treasure on an island so that when he became old he could dig it up and live off the riches for the rest of his life. However, the pirate was not so sure where that treasure was.

You see, many moons ago (and still today), the pirate was a tad impulsive and would do things like act before thinking about the consequences. This got him into many troublesome situations such as stealing, getting lost, and getting himself in the middle of swashbuckling sword fights that he never meant to get involved with.

The pirate also had trouble paying attention to details and focusing on his surroundings. This made listening to directions difficult AND made map reading a nightmare. (A word of advice—if you ever find yourself on a pirate ship, make sure the person reading the map pays attention to details or you might end up in a pit of quicksand or a shark infested area.)

The pirate was also disorganized. Even when he did take notes or draw maps, he usually lost track of them.

This meant the pirate had to find his treasure based on memory alone. He had no notes, no lists, no reminders of any kind. This was not going to be easy and he was at a loss as to what to do. So the pirate asked his friend Pete for help. Pete was well known among the pirates for paying attention to details and being organized. The pirate figured if anyone was going to help him, it would be Pete.

Pete came to the pirate's ship and listened to the pirate's dilemma. Pete sat in silence with a thoughtful look on his face for a very long time. Then he said: "I will help you, but you must help yourself, too. I will show you how to prepare for this trip and find your treasure but you have to learn a few things first." They shook hands on the deal.

The next morning Pete returned to the pirate's ship and said: "Today is your first lesson. Today you will learn to get organized." During that day Pete showed the pirate how making lists and keeping them in a special place can be helpful. For example, the pirate made one list of everything he would need to pack for his trip. He also made a list of the places and landmarks he remembered about the place where he hid his treasure.

The next day Pete showed the pirate how to map together all the pieces of information he had listed about the treasure's location. They looked at several maps and were able to narrow down the treasure's general location.

Later in the week Pete showed the pirate how to slow his mind and body down long enough to look around, stop, and think about what he needs to be doing. Pete said: "This will help you be less impulsive—it will help you make better decisions."

The pirate learned to pause and take a deep breath if he started to feel like his mind was racing.

Pete also gave the pirate some "fidgets" to help the pirate focus. The pirate placed one of the fidgets in his pocket so he would have one with him anytime he needed it. He also put a few fidgets near places he might need to stop and think for a moment. He put a piece of seaglass next to his map—this way he could rub the piece of seaglass while he studied the map. Then he went to the hull of the ship and left a periwinkle shell next to the steering wheel. That way, if the seas were calm and he started to feel distracted, he could hold onto the periwinkle and feel the curious curves of the shell to help him stay focused on steering. Finally, the pirate put a prickly sea urchin shell on the table where he left his guidebooks and important papers. That way, when he had to read something with a lot of detail, he could fidget with the urchin shell to help keep him alert and focused.

The pirate finally felt ready to take his ship out to sea in search of the treasure. He used his fidgets when he needed to focus; he practiced "stop and think" when he needed to make decisions; he used his lists to help keep him organized and to remember things he needed to get done. He followed the map he and Pete had made, and as he entered the general area in which he knew his treasure lay, he started to recognize familiar landmarks.

The pirate was able to find his treasure and return home with many riches. Now he could leave his pirate life behind and enjoy the rest of his years relaxing. He was so thankful for the help that Pete had provided him that he gave Pete a generous share of the treasure.

 ## An activity to go along with the story

COLOR "THE LOST TREASURE MAP"

Color the treasure map that the pirate lost in the story (see handout).

 ## Affirmations

✓ Today I will stop and think before I speak.

✓ Today I will stop and think before I act.

✓ Slow down.

✓ Breathe first.

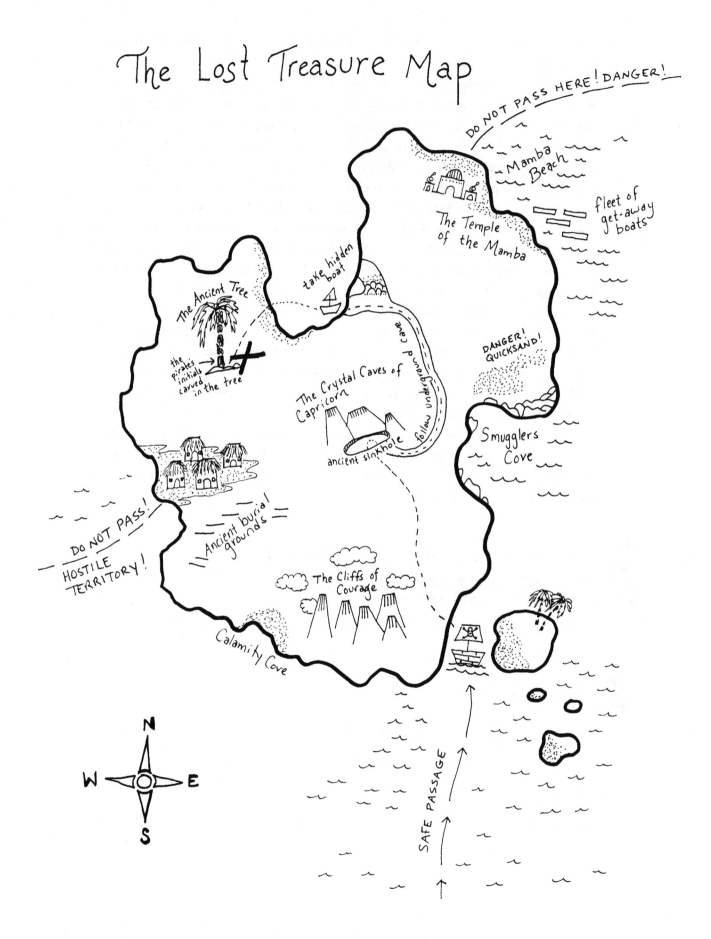

CHAPTER 6

Taming Anxiety, Stuck Thoughts, and Stuck Behaviors

. . . .

Challenges

The child worries excessively.

The child perseverates and/or has intrusive thoughts.

The child experiences anxiety and/or panic attacks.

Goals

The child will be able to put worries aside so they can do what they need to get done and/or relax.

The child will be able to stop or decrease their intrusive thoughts or actions.

The child will have at least three coping strategies for managing their worries or anxiety.

Skills: Reducing anxiety, stuck thoughts, and stuck behaviors

Skills addressed in this chapter include identifying the worry or anxiety, setting boundaries with worries, getting facts about fears, identifying areas where the child has some control building confidence around managing mistakes, practicing flexibility using guided imagery, using progressive muscle relaxation, using "grounding" skills, and planning ahead for self-care when feeling worried or anxious. Breathing and other general calming skills are also helpful for children learning to manage their worries and anxiety; these skills are addressed in Chapter 4.

Interventions

WORRY DOLLS

I write about Worry Dolls in all of my books because the clients I work with love them so much. Worry Dolls are small, handcrafted dolls that are used in various ways: the child can tell their worries to the doll; the child can write a worry on a thin strip of paper and wrap it around the doll prior to decorating it (the child practices visualizing the doll "holding onto the worry" for them); and the child can simply use the worry doll for comfort or as a transitional object of something you made together.

The dolls can be crafted to look like people, superheroes, or even animals. They can be called Worry Dolls, Worry Warriors, or a special name designated by your child or client. So as you can see, they are versatile. Here are general instructions for making a Worry Doll.

Materials

- Scissors

- Paper scraps

- Old fashioned clothespins (peg doll style)

- Fine tipped permanent markers

- Embroidery string for hair

- Glue stick

- Pipe cleaners

- Various fabric scraps and ribbon

Directions

- If the child wants to write a worry on a strip of paper and attach it to the doll, then do that first: cut a thin strip of paper and write the child's worry onto it. Glue the strip of paper around the midsection of the doll. This helps children visualize the doll actually holding onto the worry for them.

- *Face:* The child draws a face on the doll using the permanent markers.

- *Hair:* To make long hair, cut several pieces of string to the same length, gather them together side by side, then use a separate piece of string to wrap around the hair and tie a knot in the center. Glue the hair to the doll's head. To make braids, simply braid a section of strings and tie each end of the braid in a knot. Trim the braid just below each knot. Tie a string around the center of the braid if you like, and then glue the braid to the doll's head. Short hair is usually best drawn on, rather than using string. Use the permanent markers to draw the hair on.

- *Arms:* Wrap a pipe cleaner around the doll's front and then around the back, then out front again to create arms. Trim the arms to size and glue them in place. Alternatively, you can cut two small strips of pipe cleaner and glue them to each side of the doll for arms.

- *Clothing:* To make a shirt, wrap a small strip of fabric around the top of the doll. For pants, it is recommended that you wrap string in and around each leg, gluing it in place. This is tedious but does create the best "pants-like" look. For skirts and dresses, the child can wrap strips of fabric around the doll. Glue all fabric in place.

- Allow the doll to dry.

GET THE FACTS

Anxiety can stem from not knowing what to expect—it feeds on the "unknown." Children who get anxious easily tend to imagine the worst that could occur, based on fear rather than facts. Therefore, it can be helpful to list out the child's fears and address each and every one of them with factual information. Whether or not the child's fears are real or imagined, having the true facts and a plan to deal with the fear can alleviate a lot of worry.

Directions

- List the worries.

- List the coping and calming strategies that could be helpful in managing each worry.

- Write out the plan for each "what if," even if the "what if" is highly unlikely to happen.

PLAY DOUGH VS. ROCK

Materials

- Small rock

- Handful of play dough

People who are prone to anxiety can get stuck in a pattern of thinking about all of the things that could go wrong in a situation. If there is a child in your life who does this, it might help to use the Play Dough vs. Rock analogy. Here is a sample script of how I use this activity with a child:

"Some situations are like play dough—with play dough you have some control over how it gets shaped." (Demonstrate this with the handful of play dough by making a few different shapes with it.)

"Other situations are like a rock—no matter how much you squeeze or try to mold it, you cannot control the shape of it." (Demonstrate this by trying to mold a rock into a shape.) "Most situations will fit into these two categories. If you have a 'play dough situation' it means you have some choice or control in the outcome of the matter. It means you can do something to change the situation. Rock situations are those that are most likely not in your control, or even in your influence."

When children get caught up in a heap of worries, it can be helpful to go through the worries and figure out which ones are "play dough" and which ones are "rock." Here's an example:

Child: "I'm worried about getting detentions. I am marked late at school almost every day and then I get detentions for it."

Counselor: "Okay, so let's break the worry down. Let's figure out which parts of the worry are play dough and which are rock. Let's start with the school. Is the school going to change its rules about lateness?"

Child: "No."

Counselor: "I agree—that sounds like a rock situation to me because you have no immediate control over the school policy on lateness. So the next question is: Can you change anything on your end about getting to school on time?"

Child: "I guess I could get up earlier and take the bus instead of relying on my sister to drive me to school. She's always late! It's not fair that she makes me late for school and I get in trouble for it."

Counselor: "So it sounds like getting to school is a 'play dough situation' because you're saying that you have some control over this."

Kids who worry a lot need tools and support to focus their energy on what they have control over, and to let go of the rest as much as they're able. They can't worry about everything all the time or they will exhaust themselves and perpetuate an unhealthy thinking pattern. The analogy of Play Dough vs. Rocks is a tool to help them practice prioritizing where to spend their energy when it comes to worries.

PRACTICE MAKING MISTAKES

Making mistakes and learning how to handle them is an essential skill for kids to learn. But for some children, making a mistake (especially in front of others) can cause a great amount of distress, especially if the child has social anxiety, obsessions/compulsions, or low self-esteem.

There are gentle interventions you can try, however, to encourage a child to practice making mistakes and managing the outcome. When a child is practicing making mistakes, they are also practicing being flexible, managing emotions, and creating new solutions. These are all skills that help a child to make a mistake and move forward without getting stuck in anxiety, worry, shame, guilt, or feelings of inadequacy. Here are some activities that encourage making mistakes and managing the outcomes:

- *Doodling*—Doodling encourages mistakes because it's a free-form activity. Give the child one sheet of paper and a pencil and instruct them that if they draw something they don't like, either to change it into something else, or find another way to work with it.

- *Role play*—Younger kids can use puppets, dolls, stuffed animals, and/or figurines to act out scenarios that include making mistakes and managing the outcome of those mistakes.

- *Use media as a reference point*—For older youth, have a dialogue about a TV show, film, or video game in which a character makes a poor choice. How did that character deal with the outcome of their choice? What does the child think about the manner in which the character dealt with the outcome? How would the child have managed the same situation?

ROLL WITH IT

This activity focuses on the mantra "just roll with it," which means "be flexible," and provides something the child can take away from your session for a reminder to practice this skill. Anxious children tend to love predictability, but as you know, things can go askew in any given situation. Therefore, flexibility is a wonderful skill for children to practice, and eventually embrace, because it's the cornerstone for anxiety management.

"Rolling with it" can mean accepting a change in plans, coming up with an alternative plan, observing what is going on around you instead of reacting to it right away, taking a deep breath and counting to ten, embracing your curiosity to find out what happens next, etc. Rolling with it simply means you adjust in a given situation, using an open mind and flexibility.

Materials

- Roll With It activity sheet

- Markers or crayons

- Scissors

- Tape or glue

Directions

- Color the circus announcer and cut him out.

- Roll the announcer around so that he makes a circle with his body.

- Follow the arrows and directions on the coloring page and use tape or glue to attach the announcer's hands to his feet, as well as his head to his groin. This will allow the announcer to roll.

COLOR MANDALAS

Coloring calms the brain, and mandalas are one of my favorite means for coloring. Mandalas are circular images that tend to be symmetrical and they're illustrated using various themes and patterns. If your child or client loves to color, there are many mandala coloring books geared to children. The coloring books come in a variety of skill levels. Enjoy some time coloring mandalas with the child. Put on relaxing music and lower the lighting just a little if it helps the child to relax into the activity better.

*

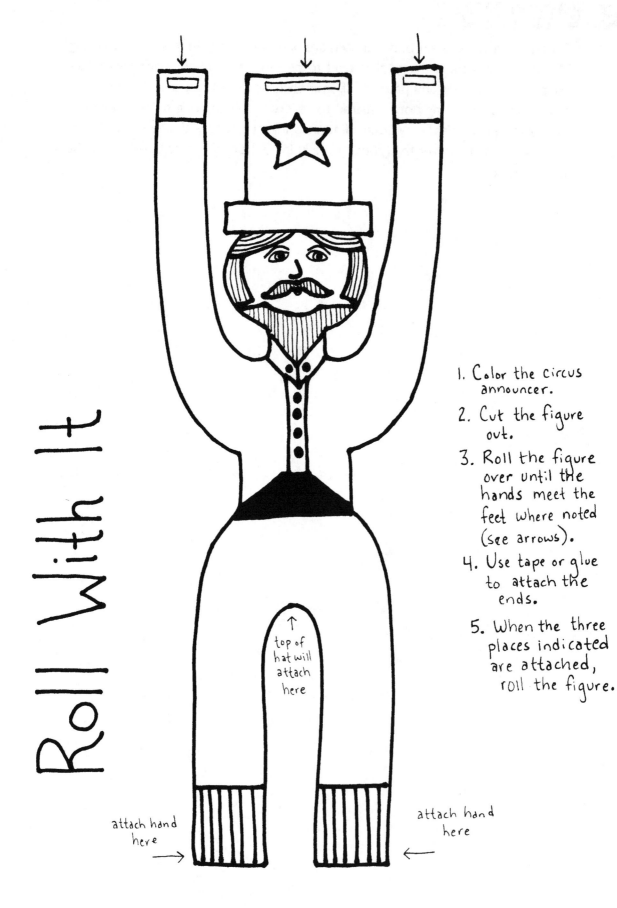

Roll With It

1. Color the circus announcer.

2. Cut the figure out.

3. Roll the figure over until the hands meet the feet where noted (see arrows).

4. Use tape or glue to attach the ends.

5. When the three places indicated are attached, roll the figure.

↑
top of hat will attach here

attach hand here →

← attach hand here

*

*

GUIDED IMAGERY

Guided Imagery is similar to storytelling, but with a focus on relaxation. A narrator describes an experience using descriptive words that help the child feel like they are experiencing the story. A Guided Imagery story can help a child relax, feel calmer or more "grounded," and even help them drift off to sleep feeling relaxed rather than worried or tense. Guided imagery books and audio are plentiful on the market—you can use your online search engine to search "guided imagery for kids" to find more resources. Here is an example of Guided Imagery.

THE RAINBOW ISLAND

Take a moment to get comfortable and then close your eyes. (PAUSE while child gets comfortable.)

You have just arrived at Rainbow Island. Step onto the dock and take a deep breath.

You will notice the dock is mostly empty and uncluttered, but there is a barrel in front of you. The barrel is where you leave your worries and the day's events behind you while you go to visit Rainbow Island.

Take a moment to think about your day. Did anything happen today that made you feel sad, confused, scared, or angry? If so, take a moment to imagine putting those experiences and feelings in the barrel. (PAUSE) Did you have any worries today? If so, put those in the barrel as well. You can put any idea, thought, feeling, or experience in the barrel. Put anything in the barrel that you'd like to leave behind for a bit. You can come back and get them at any time if you want them back. For now, though, leave them here so you can go and enjoy Rainbow Island with a light heart.

Now it is time to go explore the island. Rainbow Island is a place where you are safe and loved and cherished. It is a place that understands and honors you. You are a welcomed guest here.

Walk to the end of the dock where it meets the land. Follow the grass path up the hill. You will find a large rock there. It is big enough for you to climb on top of, if you like. You can get a beautiful view of the water from there. The rock has been in the sun all day and is warm underneath your touch. Take a moment to lie on the rock and enjoy how warm it is. Lie on your back and feel the sun on your face. Take a moment to listen to all the sounds around you. Can you hear the ocean waves in the distance? Or the birds singing from the trees? Can you hear the breeze blowing through the trees and across the grass?

When you are ready, leave the rock and keep following the path you were on before. As you walk, see if you can smell the salty air from the ocean. Or can you smell the flowers that grow wild among the grass here? The flowers smell a bit like cinnamon mixed with honey and a hint of sea roses. If you concentrate hard enough, I bet you can smell the scent of the grass, too.

As you walk along the path you will find a sign. The sign has an arrow on it and says "Rainbow Island Lighthouse." Follow the direction of the arrow. It will lead you to a lighthouse.

As you turn a slight corner, you see the lighthouse. The lighthouse tower is painted with rainbow stripes—red, orange, yellow, green, blue, indigo, and violet. There is a sign outside the tower that says "Welcome!" so you go inside.

When you step inside the lighthouse tower you are at the red level. A sign on the wall says: "You are safe and protected here."

As you walk up the stairs, the walls become orange. The sign on the orange wall says: "You are filled with joy."

Further up the stairs the walls become a bright yellow. A sign here says: "Follow your dreams. Believe in yourself."

You stop for a moment to look up—there are still a few levels to go but you do not feel tired yet, so you keep going up the lighthouse stairs.

Soon, the walls are a beautiful shade of green. A sign here says: "Love and be loved."

As you walk even further toward the top of the tower, the walls become a shade of sky blue. You notice the words "Honor your voice: speak up, and speak out" painted on the wall.

When you continue up the stairs, the sky blue walls deepen to a shade of deep blue indigo. Here there is a sign that says: "Listen to your intuition."

And finally you reach the top level of the stairs. The walls here are violet. The sign on the wall says: "You are pure love and light."

As you stand at the top of the lighthouse, you now have a view of everything—you can see the water, the land, and the sky. You see the people, the animals, the trees, and the plants. You feel connected to all of these things. And as you look out at everything, you feel your heart fill up with an abundance of love, light, and acceptance.

Take a moment to enjoy this feeling. Remember that here, at Rainbow Island, you are safe and loved. Feel that love in every part of your body. Imagine that love wrapping around you.

When you are ready, head back down the lighthouse stairs. You pass from violet, to indigo, to sky blue, to green, to yellow, to orange, and finally to red. Head back outside to the grass path and back to the large rock on the hill. Relax for a while here on the rock again until you are ready to return to the dock. If you want to bring any of your day's events with you, make sure to retrieve them from the barrel before you go. But feel free to leave them here at Rainbow Island—they will stay in the barrel until you need or want them.

Take another moment to stand on the dock and look at the beauty of Rainbow Island. Then close your eyes, feel the sun on your face, and focus on how loved and safe you are here.

Take a deep breath and open your eyes when you are ready to come back.

PROGRESSIVE MUSCLE RELAXATION

Progressive Muscle Relaxation is an intentional tensing and releasing of various muscle groups in the body. By tensing each muscle group and then purposefully releasing that tension, you encourage your mind and body to relax. When you use Progressive Muscle Relaxation, you start at one end of the body and work your way to the other—from top to bottom or bottom to top. One way to teach kids this method is to use guided imagery while instructing them which muscles to tense up and then relax.

PROGRESSIVE MUSCLE RELAXATION SCRIPT

Today we're going to try what's called "Progressive Muscle Relaxation." It sounds complicated but it's really quite simple. Progressive Muscle Relaxation means tensing and then relaxing the muscles in each part of your body. It helps the body to release tension and feel more relaxed. To help you learn how to do this, I'm going to read through a step-by-step list of instructions in the form of a story.

Use your imagination while you listen to the story and follow the instructions.

First, lie down in a comfortable position.

When you are comfortable, take a deep breath and close your eyes. Now we'll begin.

Today we are going on a journey to a land of make-believe.

Imagine you open a door and you step outside to a beautiful world filled with trees, grass, forest, mountains, flowers, and nature all around. Imagine taking your shoes off and leaving them at the door. Walk around for a moment in your bare feet and explore.

Feel the grass under your toes.

Feel the cool clay of the earth under your heels.

Now pretend you find a sticky mud puddle. Stick your feet in that mud puddle. Imagine the mud is thick and squishy and warm. Feel the mud around your ankles and toes. Now scrunch up your toes as tight as you can and feel the mud ooze between each toe. Squeeze those toe muscles! Tighten the muscles in the arch and ball of your feet as well. Count to 3. 1…2…3…and then let all that tension go. Relax your toes and feet.

Imagine there is a stream nearby. Walk over to the stream and stick your feet in it. Feel your feet relax in the cool water as it swirls around your ankles, washing your feet clean.

Now look around and find a clearing in the grass. Imagine you go over to the clearing and stand tall in the sunshine there, pretending to be a tree. The roots of the tree are your feet, the trunk is your legs and lower body, and the top of the tree is your upper body—your arms, neck, and head.

First, I want you to feel the trunk of your tree. Squeeze the muscles in your calves, then your knees, and then upper legs to make the strongest tree trunk possible. Tense those muscles and squeeze them super tight. You want your tree trunk to stand tall and strong in the forest. Count to 5. 1...2...3...4...5... Squeeze for one more moment and then release. Let go of all that tension and feel your tree trunk relax.

Now stretch your arms out. Pretend your arms are the branches of the tree and you want to reach out as far as you can. Reach, reach, reach, and stretch all those branches out. Make tight fists with your hands. Then, pretend a very large bird has come to sit on your branches. You will have to tense up those arm muscles in order to hold a bird that big. Squeeze those arm muscles tight and hold the large bird on your branches. Keep holding! It looks like that bird really loves your tree and wants to sit for a moment and enjoy it. Keep those muscles nice and strong. And just like that, the bird takes off. You can let go of that tension now. Relax all the muscles in your hands and arms. Let go of all the tension. Relax your branches and take a deep breath.

Now pretend that in the center of your tree there is a hollow. The hollow is where your stomach is. Inside the hollow there's a nest. A sleepy raccoon wants to come and take a nap here. He's a very friendly and soft raccoon, but very sleepy. As he climbs up to the nest, tense up your tummy and back muscles to hold the nest in place. Squeeze those belly muscles as the raccoon curls up inside the nest, in the hollow of the tree. Thankfully, he is a quick napper and you only have to squeeze those muscles while you count to 5. Count to 5 in your mind. 1...2...3...4...5... and then relax all those muscles in your back and stomach. Let all the tension go away from the center of your body. The raccoon has gone—he is now off to find a snack. Take a moment to feel those belly muscles relax.

Next, pretend that the whole upper part of your body—your neck and your head—are reaching up, up into the sky with all the other treetops. Stretch those neck muscles up into the sky. Hold that pose for a moment and then relax your neck. Let go of any tension you have in your neck and take a deep breath.

As you stand in the forest with the other trees, you notice a sprinkle. There are tiny drops of rain coming down from the sky. The raindrops tickle the leaves on your tree! Squeeze your eyes shut really tight—this will help to keep the rain from tickling your face. Scrunch up all of your face muscles—even your nose! Squeeze all of those muscles tight. Hold that for a few moments to the count of 3 this time. 1...2...3...and then let go. The rain stops and it is no longer tickling your face or leaves.

The sun comes out from behind a cloud and shines brightly in the forest and meadow. Imagine you are no longer a tree, but a person just enjoying the sun on your face, on a warm day. Feel the earth beneath you, supporting you. Lie here and feel how all of the muscles in your body are quiet and relaxed and loose. Your body feels calmer and at peace.

Take a few minutes to enjoy this feeling. When you are ready to come back, open your eyes and take a nice slow stretch.

GET "GROUNDED"

Grounding exercises are those that help to reduce anxiety and distress in the moment. They can be helpful for people feeling an anxiety attack coming on and for those who feel they are dissociating or experiencing a flashback. One of the quickest and easiest exercises in grounding is to tune into your current surroundings and identify three things you can feel, see, hear, and smell. This simple act helps to shift your focus to the moment and feel more "in your body."

Use the Get "Grounded" worksheet to talk about this exercise with the child. Practice it with them so they become familiar using it. Let the child know that this is a coping and calming strategy they can use at any given moment and place.

Get "Grounded"

Find 3 things you can see

What are 3 things you can smell?

What are 3 things you hear right now?

Name 3 things you can feel at the moment.

Grounding exercises are helpful when you feel anxious or distressed because they bring your attention and focus to the present moment.

SELF-CARE BOX

Find a shoebox or a plastic storage container for the child to decorate. The box can be decorated with markers, crayons, paper, glitter, stickers, etc.

Fill the box with items that help the child to calm down and feel more relaxed and in control of their body and mind. For example:

- "fidgets" (items the child can manipulate in their hands for self-soothing, e.g. a flip book, a tactile object, an elastic or rubber band, a glitter filled wand)

- worry stone

- special crystal or gem

- photo of a place that the child finds calming

- stress ball to squeeze

- stack of post-it notes and mini markers for drawing or writing how the child feels

- small journal

- quotes or words of inspiration

- worksheets or coloring pages

When the child is feeling upset, unsure, frazzled, worried, anxious, or just having a tough time, bring out the box and provide some quiet time for them to use what they need to feel calmer.

MY ANXIETY SCALE

Use the My Anxiety Scale handout as a way to describe and measure a child's anxiety symptoms. Write down the calming and coping strategies that best help the child when they are feeling anxious. There is a small space on the handout to add this information. The child can keep a copy of the handout for reference and as a reminder for how they manage their own anxiety symptoms at various stages of symptoms.

TIPS FOR MANAGING ANXIETY ATTACKS

When you're an adult trying to comfort a child who is feeling anxious (or if the anxious child is able to read), having a short list of calming strategies can be a welcome resource. The following handout provides helpful suggestions and reminders for ways to minimize and manage anxiety.

*

My Anxiety Scale

1   I'm not feeling anxious at all.

2   I'm not sure if I'm feeling any anxiety. If I am, it's not getting in the way of what I want to do, or need to do.

3   I'm feeling a little anxious. Here are some things I can do to lower my anxiety at this level:

_____

_____

_____

4   I feel anxious. Here are some things I can do to lower my anxiety at this level:

_____

_____

_____

5   I'm having an anxiety attack / panic attack. This is my plan for what to do when I'm having this feeling:

_____

_____

_____

_____

Tips for Managing Anxiety Attacks

Have a plan ahead of time for how you will manage an anxiety attack if you have one again. Some children have more than one plan (e.g. one for school, one for summer camp, one for home). Look at the ideas below and highlight or underline the ones you think will help.

Also, make sure your teacher, school nurse, and other providers know that you have a history of having anxiety so they can help you if/when it happens. Make a plan ahead of time for how others can be most supportive to you. For example: Tim feels better knowing that he has a card in his desk he can hand to his teacher if he is experiencing anxiety. He gives the card to his teacher and the teacher knows he will walk to the school nurse or take a bathroom break to feel calmer and take care of his needs.

Tips

- Recognize that you are having an anxiety attack: "I'm having an anxiety attack. I have been through this before and I know it will pass. Until it passes I have some things I can do to help me get through it."

- Breathe in to the count of 4, breathe out to the count of 4. Or use a breathing technique that works best for you.

- Get a drink of water.

- Imagine yourself in a calm, relaxing, safe space.

- Talk to someone supportive.

- Try lying on the floor with your legs against the wall. You will feel less light-headed that way.

*

- Listen to a meditation or guided imagery piece (you can buy and/or listen to these in many forms including CDs, apps, iTunes, and YouTube).

- Snuggle a pet.

- Try physical activity to burn off the extra adrenaline.

- Distract yourself by doing something you typically enjoy.

- Add other strategies and interventions here:

_____

_____

_____

_____

_____

_____

_____

_____

_____

_____

_____

_____

_____

_____

_____

_____

An accompanying story
The Coat with Many Pockets

Roxy was a little girl who had many worries. She worried about her alarm not waking her up. She worried about getting a bellyache if she ate breakfast too early in the morning. She worried about getting to the bus on time. She worried about losing her snack at school. She worried about…just about everything. This was exhausting for Roxy. She didn't want to worry about everything.

One day Roxy came to school and her teacher wasn't there. Instead, there was a substitute teacher. Roxy immediately started to worry—what if the substitute teacher was mean? What if this teacher decided to do things differently than her regular teacher? What if this teacher didn't know what to do in a fire drill? What if, what if, what if? Roxy was suddenly very anxious.

The substitute teacher must have seen the worry on Roxy's face. She came right over to Roxy and said: "Hello, I'm Mrs. Meyers. I'm going to be your teacher for today. Who are you?"

Roxy told Mrs. Meyers her name.

"It's nice to meet you, Roxy!"

When Roxy's classmates arrived to class, Mrs. Meyers made an announcement. She told the students that she understood that having a substitute teacher can be difficult for some kids to adjust to, even if it's for one day. She noted that she had brought her special coat, though, which had a pocket for anyone who wanted to put a worry in it. In fact, the coat had many pockets!

Mrs. Meyers pointed to a coat hanging on the coat hook near her desk.

"If any of you have something you are feeling nervous or worried about, feel free to write or draw it on a piece of paper and then put it in one of the pockets. The coat will hold onto those worries for you so that you don't have to hold onto them! And if there is a certain worry you want or need me to know about right away, put it in this special pocket with the rainbow on it."

Roxy was intrigued by this coat with many pockets. She started writing down worries right away and tucking them into the coat. She added worries through the morning. But by lunchtime she noticed something—she wasn't worrying so much. It seemed that by writing all her worries down and putting them away in the pockets, Roxy was letting go of her worries, even if it was just for a little bit. Roxy found this to be relaxing. She liked feeling relaxed.

As the day moved on, Roxy suddenly had a worried thought—what will she do with her worries tomorrow if Mrs. Meyers is not at school? Roxy immediately wrote this worry down and put it in the special rainbow pocket.

A little later, Mrs. Meyers read the worry and went over to Roxy to let her know she had an idea. They would talk about it at snack time.

At snack time Mrs. Meyers gave all of the kids a piece of paper. She told them to fold it in half and use staples or tape to seal the sides. She told the kids this would be their own personal "pocket" that they could put their worries in. That way, they would not need Mrs. Meyers' Coat with Many Pockets—they could have a pocket of their own.

Roxy loved this idea. She made many different pockets and put them on her bedroom wall so she could add to them whenever she wanted. She even made a special rainbow pocket to remind her of Mrs. Meyers.

 ## An activity to go along with the story

A POCKET FOR MY WORRIES

Materials

- Paper
- Stapler
- Markers
- Tape
- Scissors

Directions

- Fold a piece of paper in half.

- Add staples along the sides and the crease of the folded paper to create a "pocket." The staples will look like stitches on a pocket.

- Decorate the pocket with various designs.

- Add tape around the edges of the pocket if you want to cover the staples. I do this with clients who are likely to pick at the staples.

- Write your worries on strips of paper and put them in the pocket. As you put these worries in the pocket, imagine letting go of them.

✔ Affirmations

- ✔ Roll with it.
- ✔ It's okay to make mistakes.
- ✔ Let go.
- ✔ Be flexible.
- ✔ I'm okay.

CHAPTER 7

Social Anxiety and Selective Mutism

⚠ Challenges

The child is sensitive to environments, shy, quiet, introverted, selectively mute.

The child doesn't talk in front of others, except for family.

The child gets embarrassed easily when they become the center of attention.

◎ Goals

The child will be able to communicate their needs when they need or want to.

The child will use alternative means to communicate to others.

The child will have at least one good friend they will talk to.

It's important that adults understand the difference between a child who is quiet or introverted vs. a child who has aspects of social anxiety. Quieter children are typically content with one or two friends and can present as being shy, reserved, and even stand-offish. Children with social anxiety, however, desire the social interaction but cannot act on those desires to interact with others because anxiety gets in the way.

If you are parenting or providing care for a child who seems more introverted, I recommend reading and researching about the wonderful gifts that introverted people possess and provide. If, on the other hand, the child is experiencing distress or is not able to function in some capacity (e.g. the child doesn't speak to anyone outside the home), you may want to consult a professional.

Working with children who are too anxious or shy to speak to others can present unique challenges for counselors and other supportive professionals because we are so used to engaging kids in *verbal* discussion about their feelings and needs. Discussions, though, may not be an option with these children if they are too anxious or shy to speak in the first place. Some of these children may even find nonverbal communication too overwhelming.

When you first start meeting with a child who has social anxiety, shyness, or selective mutism, the key (in my opinion) is to get the child familiar with you and your space. It's not about getting the child to talk, even though that may be the long-term goal. As the child becomes accustomed to the routine and familiarity of coming to see you, you can start to employ some other interventions that encourage verbal communication, but do not require it.

Skills: Social anxiety and selective mutism

Skills addressed in this chapter include honoring and understanding the needs of quieter children, identifying alternate means of communication, creating a tiered system for adjusting to new places, and creating quiet spaces where the child can take breaks if needed.

Interventions

STEPPING STONES

Starting at a new daycare or school can be especially challenging for children who are shy, anxious, mute, and/or do not tolerate transitions well. When I work with children who have trouble adjusting to new faces and places, I employ the Stepping Stones approach, which means breaking a goal down into smaller steps. In this case, the goal is that the child will start a new daycare or school with minimal stress. Look over the Stepping Stones handout to see how this larger goal is broken down into smaller steps.

The same approach can be used for other transitions (such as moving to a new home, starting a new grade in school, introducing a child to parent's new partner).

Stepping Stones

Tips and stages for helping children adjust to a new setting and/or a new care provider (e.g. counselor, school, doctor)

Parent/guardian informs the child about the new care provider—For example: "In three weeks you will be starting preschool."

Parent/guardian answers any of the child's questions about the new care provider.

Parent/guardian identifies the building or location where new care provider will be. For example, while driving home from errands, Mom points out to the child that the building next to the post office is where the child will be starting preschool.

Parent/guardian drives around the parking area of the building to get a closer look and allow the child to see the surroundings of the exterior space.

Parent/guardian arranges a visit at the new care provider's space. The new care provider is there to say hello to the child *and then allows child and family to explore the grounds, classroom, office, etc. on their own.* NOTE: For children who are selectively mute or extremely quiet, this is a critical step. The hope (and the goal) is that this step is repeated, if necessary, until the child is comfortable talking to parents/guardians on site. This gives the child the actual experience of NOT being anxious about speaking on the premises, thereby creating some familiarity and comfort around the fact she has already communicated verbally to others here, even if it's only been to a parent. Of course, some organizations may not be flexible with this step, for various reasons. If that is the case, move on to the next step.

Arrange a short but fun visit with the care provider—parents remain present for this meeting. This could be a 15-minute visit where the care provider and child play a quick game, have a snack or tea party, or the care provider engages the child in a fun activity. Keep this visit short and sweet. If the child does not engage at all with the care provider, the parent and care provider can engage the child together. If the child is still hesitant to join in, provide the child with a parallel play activity while parent and provider continue with the planned activity for the remaining few minutes.

Check in—how is your child managing the transition thus far? Have a discussion with the child about what is working and not working thus far. Remember—the short-term goal is to create a transition that allows the child to get used to a new setting. The long-term goal is for the child to be able to speak up and express their needs in that setting. At this point, you are checking in about how the child feels about the new setting and what their worries are, if any, about the transition and the new care provider.

Create Conversation Cards (see page 142). Have a discussion with your child about what cards may be needed for the new care provider. Create these cards based on the child's needs for that care provider and/or make a set of general cards that are universal to any care provider they would go to.

Have a final meeting at the new care provider's if necessary. The parent can go over any remaining concerns and planning, the care provider can interact more with the child, everyone can go over the Conversation Cards and/or come up with additional strategies for engaging the child. Possible strategies to consider:

- The child arrives ten minutes earlier than the other kids to ease into the routine and have brief 1:1 time with the care provider to encourage more familiarity and communication.

- The child is assigned jobs that do not involve speaking but still encourage interaction (e.g. passing out napkins at snack time).

- The child has a designated staff person or space to go to if feeling overwhelmed.

Provide incentive charts if needed for attendance. This rewards the child for showing up, even if the child is not able to participate in the routine yet. Establish new charts as the child improves (e.g. the child earns an incentive for joining peers at circle time). When joining circle time has become routine for the child, then a new goal and incentive is added. This continues until the child is participating fully (or to the best of their ability) in each part of the daily routine.

CREATING QUIET SPACES

Children who are quiet, introverted, shy, and/or anxious often need a quiet space to retreat to if they are feeling overwhelmed. If at all possible, create a small space in your office or home for a child to "get away" and have some quiet. It could be a "curtained-off" area, such as putting a blanket over a desk, making a teepee or meditation station, creating a blanket or pillow fort, or designing a small nook where the child has access to favorite books or a calming kit.

SHHHHHH

When the quiet or selectively mute child has started to develop a relationship with you and/or is starting to use more nonverbal and verbal language with you, Shhhhhh can be a fun game. The rules of the game are basically to be quiet. The first person to make a noise loses the game. Now, this may not sound like much fun, or like much of a game. However, children who are quiet by nature are constantly pushed to speak up and NOT be quiet. In our extroverted, fast-paced cultures, silence is underrated. Shhhhhh is a game that honors that strength of being silent or quiet. It's a gentle confidence booster for the child.

That being said, the game can also be altered to help the child become more vocal or engaged. I know one child and counselor who played Shhhhhh and ended up in a fit of giggles (from both of them). It started when the counselor sneezed while playing the game. The counselor used the moment to exaggerate the sneeze, making it silly. The child had been engaged with the counselor over weeks now, and they had a good relationship. The child had been mute the entire time. But when the counselor sneezed in that silly exaggerated way, the child started to giggle and the counselor did too. From then on, when they played this game, they would pretend they were going to sneeze to try and get the other to laugh. This helped the child to start being more vocal (via laughing) and eventually be able to start speaking to the counselor.

 ## An accompanying story

The Quiet Giant

Once upon a time, there was a village called Boom—it was named for the very loud giants who inhabited the town. Residents from the neighboring towns often said the giants had loud, booming voices that carried all across the valley and into their homes. And when the giants walked nearby, the ground would shake and make deep grumbly "boom boom boom" sounds with every step they took.

Booming voices, booming footsteps—these giants were very loud indeed.

Then one day, a baby giant was born. A quiet giant. The baby giant didn't cry. The baby giant didn't fuss or scream. The baby giant didn't hiccup, or burp, or even boom the littlest bit. This baby giant didn't boom in the least! The parents didn't know what to do. Was something wrong with their baby?

The parents brought the baby to every doctor they knew. They wanted to know why their baby wasn't loud like the others. But each doctor said the same thing: "Your baby is fine. Yes, he is more quiet than the other giants, but he is just as smart, just as sweet, and just as healthy as all the other little giants."

As the baby grew, the parents realized that the doctors were right all along. Their little giant was not loud like the others, but he was just as smart, just as sweet, and just as healthy as all the others.

But there was still a conundrum. There were times when the quiet giant didn't know what to do about being so quiet.

One time, he went to the playground and wanted to play with other giants, but he couldn't find his voice to speak up. His voice worked at home, but many times it didn't work in other places. So, he decided to try something new.

The quiet giant made a little message. The message was written on a small piece of paper. The message read: "Sometimes I cannot find my voice and I'm quiet. But I do want to play, even if I don't speak. Can I play with you?" And he kept the message in his pocket for days when he went to the playground or other public places.

As time went on, the message worked really well to help the quiet giant tell others what he needed or wanted to do. He learned to make other messages, too. And something strange started to happen. He started to feel more comfortable about playing with other giants, even the extra loud ones. Before he knew it, he didn't need to use the message cards anymore. There were even moments when the quiet giant was asked to quieten down! He was still (and always) the quietest giant that Boom had ever known, but he made a huge impact on the village. He taught the other giants about honoring each other's differences, and he was proud of himself for doing so.

 ## An activity to go along with the story

MAKE CONVERSATION CARDS

Conversation Cards are cards placed on a ring that the child can carry with them when they head to school or another community setting. The cards contain basic information that the child can share with others and/or asks questions the child may need to ask.

Materials

- Paper

- Permanent markers

- Access to a lamination machine (if you do not have access to a lamination machine use cardstock in place of paper)

- Paper hole punch

- Metal connector ring (found in office supply stores)

Directions

- Cut the paper or cardstock into equal-sized rectangles. A general guideline for size is about 2½ x 3½ in (6 x 9 cm) or the size of a playing card.

- Write statements and questions on the cards, making sure they are written at your child's reading level. If the child is not reading yet, add a visual to the card as well. Add one statement or question per card (e.g. "I need to see the nurse"—with a picture of the nurse, if necessary).

- Laminate the cards and cut them out.

- Punch a hole on the top left of each card—as close to the same spot as possible.

- Put the metal ring through the hole in each card and then close the ring.

Example cards

Sometimes it's helpful to start the cards with one card explaining why the child is using them (e.g. "Emma has difficulty speaking up—she uses these cards to help her communicate with others").

Cards for school

- May I go to the bathroom?

- I don't know where I'm supposed to be.

- My teacher's name is…

- Yes.

- No.

- Do you want to play with me?

- I need to see the nurse.

- I don't feel well.

- I got hurt.

- I need help with this.

- I can't find my homework/lunch/mittens/coat, etc.

- I feel upset.

Cards for care providers (a nanny, babysitter, daycare provider)

- I'm hungry.

- I'm thirsty.

- I don't feel well.

- I'm tired.

- Can we go outside to play?

- I need help with something—come here and I will show you.

- I'm upset.

- What is my schedule for the rest of the day?

- Yes.

- No.

- I don't want to.

- Can we do something different?

 Affirmation

✓ I can find other ways to let others know what I think and feel.

CHAPTER 8

Improving Sleep

· ·

! Challenges

The child has trouble falling asleep and/or staying asleep.

The child's "wheels keep on turning" at bedtime.

◎ Goals

The child will be following a bedtime routine.

The child will get at least _____ hours of sleep each night.

✷ Skill: Improving sleep

Sleep is critical for mental and physical health, and many children have difficulty getting a good night's sleep on a consistent basis. This chapter provides helpful skills for improving sleep via using calming skills at bedtime, using visualization to manage busy thoughts and bedtime fears, and using a combination of journaling and visualization to reduce scary dreams.

✚ Interventions

BEDSIDE BASKET

A Bedside Basket is a basket or box that sits next to the child's bed and is filled with items to encourage the child to settle in at bedtime. Bedtime items can include anything from a book to read, a coloring book and crayons, a security object, a fun flashlight, relaxation music, relaxation cards, a worry stone, worry dolls, or any other items that might help the child to relax and/or help them stay in bed until they are tired enough to fall asleep.

Add or remove objects from the basket as necessary over time to ensure that the child has a balance of items that are always in the basket (for security and consistency) as well as new items now and then that encourage the child to stay interested in using the basket.

DREAM JOURNAL

A Dream Journal is a journal devoted to keeping track of the child's dreams. Initially you may wonder why this is helpful, as children's dreams can seem rather random or odd. But sometimes you can find patterns in a child's dreams that can provide helpful information. A Dream Journal allows you to track the child's dreams for a while to see if there are repeated themes, feelings, characters, or objects.

When you or the child record details of a dream, tag a feeling to the dream. For example: This dream made me feel nervous and worried.

Sometimes dreams offer us insight into the struggles we are managing in our waking lives. For example, some children have dreams that evoke feelings of worry before and/or after a transition. Overall, the Dream Journal provides supportive information that gives you clues into ways to support the child during the day.

The journal can be anything from folded paper stapled together to a notebook or purchased journal. The child can draw or write pictures of dreams from the night before. The parent can also write down any dreams the child talks about, especially if the child is not reading or writing yet.

NIGHTMARE JOURNAL

A Nightmare Journal is similar to a Dream Journal in design, but the content is different. The only dreams that go into the Nightmare Journal are the scary or upsetting dreams. I also add envelopes to the journal so that kids can fold up their pictures or writings and seal them in the envelopes. Some children may want a lock on the journal, as well. I've had clients who are afraid of their nightmares coming back out of the journal, and in this regard, the envelopes and a lock seem to quell those fears.

I find these journals helpful because it's healthy for the child to "purge" the dream, so to speak, by putting words or images to it. In essence, the journal is a tool to help you and the child find a way to express thoughts and feelings about the nightmares. When the child processes their dream, they take away a bit of the fear because they shift from an emotional reaction to an analytical approach.

The journal can also be used to practice visualization. For example: "Use your imagination to picture trapping your nightmares into this journal so that they cannot bother you again. Draw or write about the nightmare on a page in the journal, or hide it in one of the envelopes glued to a page in the book. Imagine that when you close the journal shut, the nightmare goes far away where it can't frighten you anymore."

THE PROTECTORS OF SLEEP

The Protectors of Sleep is another activity where the child uses visualization and imagination to ward off bedtime fears. The job of the Protector of Sleep is to watch over the child while they are sleeping, and protect them from scary thoughts and dreams during the night.

The child chooses one or more Protectors of Sleep, based on the type of protection they prefer. They can choose a warrior if they want their protector to have a shield and sword to battle any bad dreams; they can choose a mermaid or wizard if they prefer magic for protection; or they can choose a spirit owl or spirit bear for animal protection. Of course, you and the child can design your very own Protectors of Sleep!

Have a discussion about what the child thinks or dreams about at night that keeps them awake or frightened. Then, have a discussion where you briefly explain that visualization is a tool that helps the brain, and the rest of the nervous system, to feel calmer and less afraid. The Protectors of Sleep are not magic and they do not have power on their own—the child has to do their own part to make the Protectors of Sleep most powerful. The child's job is to use their imagination to visualize the Protectors keeping them safe from fears and bad dreams. If the child is lying in bed and starts to worry about the shadow on the wall, they then use their imagination to bring the Protectors of Sleep to their aid. They might imagine, for example, that the Mermaid has a magical sea star that tames all the scary shadows. Or maybe the child imagines that the Spirit Owl wraps its wings around and keeps them safe from any bad dreams. The more the child can visualize feeling protected from these fears and dreams, the better they get at warding them off.

When you have colored, drawn, or created your Protectors of Sleep, place a *battery-operated* tea light in the bottom of the tube. The child can use the Protectors as a nightlight too, when necessary.

Materials

- The accompanying Protectors of Sleep coloring pages (or plain paper if you want to create your own)

- Markers, crayons, and/or colored pencils

- Scissors

- Glue

- Recycled toilet paper tubes (or other wide-mouthed cardboard tube)

- *Battery-operated* tea light

Directions

- Choose a Protector of Sleep or design your own.

- Color it and cut it out.

- Apply glue to the back of the image.

- Wrap the image around the toilet paper tube.

- Place the Protector/s of Sleep near the child's bed.

- Insert a battery-operated tea light in the bottom of the tube.

PROTECTORS OF SLEEP.....

WARRIOR

WIZARD

SPIRIT BEAR

FLASHLIGHT HACKS

Flashlight Hacks are pieces of paper that fit on the lens of a flashlight and have various shapes and designs cut from them. When you shine your flashlight toward a wall, the image is cast on the wall. "Hacked flashlights" can be used to encourage children to have fun playing with light and dark, which is helpful in desensitizing the child to a fear of the dark.

Materials

- Paper

- Scissors

- Paper hole punch

- Flashlight

Directions

- Cut paper circles to fit on the lens of a flashlight.

- Then use a paper hole punch to punch shapes in the paper such as "superhero symbols" or constellations.

- You can also cut out shapes of paper and apply those directly to the flashlight lens.

LAVENDER SPRAY

Lavender is a flower and herb that has a calming effect on people. This is why lavender oil is a popular choice in natural and/or alternative sleep aids. You can make your own lavender spray for a fraction of the cost of buying it.

Materials

- Lavender essential oil

- 4 oz (120 ml) spray bottle (these can be purchased at whole food stores or drug stores)

- 1 tsp isopropyl alcohol

- Distilled or purified water

Directions

- Add 20 drops of the lavender essential oil to the spray bottle.

- Add the isopropyl alcohol.

- Top up the spray bottle with the water.

- Shake the bottle gently to allow the ingredients to combine.

- Do a test spray—if the child does not like the smell of lavender, or if the child has an allergic reaction to it, you want to make sure this is discovered prior to spraying the child's bedroom and linens.

- Spray the child's bed linens and/or spray in the child's room before bed. This can be a comforting ritual for children to do.

Note: It is not advisable to call this "Monster Spray," because then it sounds like you are agreeing that there are indeed monsters.

 ## An accompanying story
Circus Clean Up

The circus is an exciting place to be. Have you ever been to a circus?

This story is about a young man named Timothy. Timothy had a very important job with a travelling circus—his job was to clean up the circus ring and take the tent down each and every night. It was hard work!

During afternoons and evenings the circus tent would be filled with benches and spectators. The ringmaster would come out to the center of the ring and announce each of the circus acts in his big booming voice: "Now introducing our latest performer—a woman flying from a cannon!"

"Next we will watch as two blindfolded men walk a tight rope 30 feet up in the air!"

"Let's hear some applause for our next performers—a flying trapeze trio!"

"Coming up next…the hula hooping juggling librarian"…and so on. This would go on during the day and into the evening. Eventually, the ringmaster would announce the final act—the grand finale. The grand finale meant that all the circus performers would come out at once and do many tricks at the same time—it was very exciting! After much cheering and applause, the spectators would pack up their things and head back to their homes.

This is when Timothy's job started—his job was to clean up and take the circus tent down. Timothy had done this so many times that by now he had a routine. His job actually reminded him of what it was like to go to bed each night. Timothy was the kind of person who had a busy mind—he was always thinking about things, and sometimes he had trouble quieting his mind before bed. This made it difficult for him to fall asleep. The circus was a lot like the thoughts in his mind—so many things going on at once, all of them exciting and interesting. Sometimes he even got the same thought stuck in his head (but this was not so fun). Timothy realized that going to sleep was like cleaning up after the circus—he had to put each thought and each part of the day to bed in order to clean up his mind enough to be able to sleep. This is how Timothy would do it:

Timothy would brush his teeth, put on his pajamas, get a sip of water, and get comfortable in his bed. Then, each time a thought or idea came into his mind, he would imagine himself saying goodnight to it and putting it to bed. Sometimes the thought or idea would pop back into his head, and Timothy would imagine himself saying: "We can think about this tomorrow but right now it's time for you to go to bed." And, once again, he would imagine tucking that thought into bed and saying goodnight.

At first, Timothy found this challenging. But after many nights of practice his brain started to listen better when Timothy told his thoughts to go to bed.

Cleaning up the circus taught Timothy a lot about quieting his mind enough to sleep.

An activity to go along with the story

PUTTING WORRY THOUGHTS TO BED

Worry Thoughts are those that include:

- Things I didn't get done today.

- Things I need to get done tomorrow.

- What terrible things could happen tomorrow?

- Why did I do that, say that, act that way when…?

- Did I upset or anger someone today? Did I hurt someone's feelings?

- All the bad thoughts and worries about every possible calamity and harm that could come to you and your loved ones.

Bedtime is a classic time when these Worry Thoughts become intrusive. One way to practice quieting these thoughts is to visualize a large room with many beds. Each time a worry thought comes into your head, pretend it is a sweet and harmless character such as a kitten, a puppy, or a panda cub. Imagine tucking that character into bed and saying: "Now is not the time to be worrying about these things. Now is the time to quiet your body and mind and go to sleep." If a new Worry Thought pops into your head, create a new character for it. Then imagine tucking that one into bed, the same as before. When characters get forgetful and decide to get out of bed and come bother you, imagine walking them back to their room and tucking them back into bed.

Affirmations

✓ I am safe.

✓ I will allow my body to get the rest it needs.

✓ Relax.

✓ My mind and body are calm.

CHAPTER 9

Sadness and Depression

. . . .

! Challenges

The child is unhappy much of the time.

The child is often lacking in energy and unmotivated.

The child frequently complains of feeling unloved or that people dislike them.

The child often isolates themself.

◎ Goals

The child will identify and feel moments of love, joy, or gratitude.

The child will feel connected to at least one other person.

The child will be able to identify at least two enjoyable healthy activities.

The child will not be isolating themself from people or activities that they used to enjoy.

✷ Skills: Sadness and depression

Skills addressed in this chapter include daily practice of writing in a gratitude journal, recognizing positive moments, identifying inspirations and goals, reframing situations, using visualization, and rating symptoms for monitoring.

✚ Interventions

GRATITUDE JOURNALS

Gratitude Journals are books used for keeping track of things you feel grateful for each day. Many people set a journaling goal. For example: "I will list three things I am grateful for every day." The activity is a tool for increasing positive thinking. By taking time daily to recognize and label the things for which you are grateful, you train your brain to find the positive in each day. Some days might be easy to write about. Difficult days will be more challenging (these days may result in writing about the basics for which you are thankful—a roof over your head or a meal to eat). The more consistent you are with the Gratitude Journal, the easier it becomes to identify positive moments or things.

When a child starts a Gratitude Journal, you might hear feedback that "it's not working" or "it doesn't help me." A Gratitude Journal is a daily practice that takes time before the child starts to recognize the positive benefits. Keep encouraging the child to stick with it. You can facilitate the practice by having the child identify the things or moments they are appreciative of and writing them in the journal for the child.

Many people with depression, melancholy, or dysthymia (persistent depression) will have a skewed and cloudy outlook about their daily experiences. The beauty of a Gratitude Journal is that you can go back to each day and "see" that there were still beautiful moments or things to be thankful for, even in the midst of that sadness.

The journals can be as creative or traditional as the child likes—some children are happy with handmade blank books created from pieces of paper that have been folded or stapled together. Other kids will want a sturdier journal, such as a composition notebook or blank sketchbook.

Encourage the child to decorate the cover of their journal. Collages and drawings work well for journal covers. You can also photocopy the journal cover page and accompanying images included in this book—the child can decorate the images as they wish, cut out the parts they want to use, and then glue them to the cover or pages of their journal.

Children who are learning to recognize and identify gratitude will need support and prompting to help them get started with their journals. In addition, if the child is not writing yet, you can offer to do the writing for them, or suggest they draw a picture in place of words.

Set a goal with the child to complete the journal each day for at least a month. Offer your support if the child wants or needs it. This could be reminding them to get it done, help with writing or drawing, or coming up with questions to help the child identify the high points of the day and things they are grateful for. At the end of the month, go over it together. Is the child surprised by any particular days or themes?

The following pages can be used to decorate your Gratitude Journal cover and/or pages. The Gratitude Flower can also be filled out to add to your journal, or used as a separate activity.

VISION BOARDS

A Vision Board is a visual representation of your hopes, dreams, wishes, goals, and words or quotes that inspire you. The boards can be any combination of words and images.

Vision Boards can be especially helpful for children who are struggling with depression or depressive symptoms. For these children, Vision Boards are a beautiful reminder of the things the child connects to and enjoys when not feeling depressed.

Materials

- Magazines and catalogues that are age-appropriate (nature, geography, travel, toy catalogues)

- Other possible items: stickers; photographs; a card from a favorite friend or relative; images printed from the internet (with adult supervision); a favorite candy or snack wrapper; a pretend ticket to an event the child would like to go to; a map of a place the child would like to visit someday

- Scissors

- Large poster board or a folded, accordion-style foam board

- Glue

- Markers, crayons, and/or ink pens

Directions

- Have the child look through the magazines and cut out any images or words that feel inspiring.

- Gather all of the images, words, and other items from the materials list that the child wants to add to the Vision Board.

- When the child is ready to glue the images to the Vision Board, be on standby to assist if necessary. The child might need help organizing the images to make sure they fit.

- When all of the items have been glued to the Vision Board, find a location to hang or display it where the child will see it on a regular basis.

*

My Gratitude Journal

Things I will write about in this journal:
- things, people, and places I love
- moments I've enjoyed
- nice things others have done for me or said to me
- yummy food I've had
- people and pets I care about
- good friends I've had
- things that make me smile or laugh
- special occasions, holidays, or celebrations I enjoy
- movies, games, apps, and TV that I love
- music I enjoy
- things that inspire me

*

Hope Joy
Love Peace
Courage
Safe Calm
Healthy
Inspired
Strong Smart

FILL EACH FLOWER PETAL WITH SOMETHING THAT YOU ARE GRATEFUL FOR! I AM GRATEFUL FOR THESE THINGS: FILL EACH FLOWER PETAL WITH SOMETHING THAT

*

CATERPILLAR AND BUTTERFLY THAUMATROPE

A thaumatrope is an optical illusion toy made from two images. The images are placed back to back on the top of a pencil or dowel. If you hold the pencil in your hand and rub your hands back and forth, the two images will combine into one.

A Caterpillar and Butterfly Thaumatrope can serve as a visual metaphor for children going through a challenging event. When I make these toys with children, I say something along these lines: "Do you know what happens to caterpillars? They turn into butterflies. But before they turn into butterflies they have to go through a challenging transition. I'm not even sure if the caterpillars understand why they are struggling and going through such a change. They just listen to their instincts. Their instincts tell them to prepare for a change, so they build a cocoon and they stay in there, alone and seemingly separated from the rest of the world. If the caterpillar had human feelings, I wonder what it would feel. Would it feel anxious? Scared? Excited? Lonely? What do you think?

"But then—after a period of time being inside the cocoon, it suddenly emerges as a butterfly. The caterpillar has been completely transformed. It now has wings. It can fly. It can explore a whole new world that it couldn't before. Its life has become radically different!

"When we, as people, go through really tough times, it's like being a caterpillar— we have no idea what is coming next or what is going to happen. But we have to keep going. When we get to the other side of the tough time, we are transformed. We have gained new experience and insight. The experience can make us stronger, wiser, and more beautiful."

Materials

- Caterpillar and Butterfly Thaumatrope images

- Crayons or markers

- Scissors

- Glue

- A pencil or dowel

Directions

- Have the child color the images for the thaumatrope—make sure the child uses the same background color for both images.

- Cut the circles out.

- Glue the images back to back onto the pencil or dowel.

- Allow the glue to dry.

- Roll the pencil or dowel back and forth in your hand until you see the two images become one.

Caterpillar And Butterfly
Thaumatrope

1. Cut the circles out.
2. Color them in (but use the same background color for each circle).

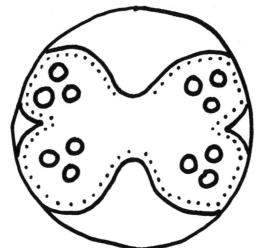

3. Tape the circles, back to back, to the top of a dowel or pencil. Make sure the butterfly wings are horizontal (as pictured).
4. Roll the dowel/pencil between your hands and watch the caterpillar become a butterfly!!

VISUALIZATION TO REMEMBER JOY

The following is a script for a visualization exercise called "Holding onto Joy." Before reading the script to the child, have them get comfortable and explain that you will be reading a brief list of instructions. All the child needs to do is listen and use their imagination as they follow the visualization. It is best if the child can close their eyes, but it is not required.

HOLDING ONTO JOY

Before we begin, start by taking a deep breath. (Take a deep breath with the child.)

Now I want you to take a moment and think about a time when your heart was happy and filled with joy. It could be a special day with someone you care about. It could be a celebration, such as a birthday or holiday. It could be a time when you received a special gift from someone. It could be something you accomplished and felt proud of. It could be a hug from someone you love. It could be a special place you like to visit.

Choose one of those moments when your heart felt happy and full of joy.

Give me a "thumbs up" when you have chosen a happy and joyful moment.

(When the child gives you the thumbs up, proceed.)

Now I want you to imagine walking into a room and finding a beautifully wrapped gift. The gift is wrapped in a box decorated with gorgeous paper and satiny ribbon. The gift is about the size of your hand. You walk closer to the gift and hold onto it.

Imagine you start to open the gift. Picture yourself untying the satiny ribbon, letting it fall to the floor. Imagine tearing off the wrapping paper, being as neat or as messy as you like. Under all of that beautiful wrapping is a box with a lid. Lift the lid and peek inside.

Imagine you find your moment of joy inside this box. Picture your heart filling up with light and warmth as the joy and happiness of that moment swirl around you.

Anytime you need to remember what joy feels like, go back to your gift and open it up. Remind yourself that joy is a gift even if it only lasts a few seconds. The beauty of this gift is that you can remember it whenever you like. Whenever you feel sad, tired, depressed, or low, remember your gift. Imagine yourself opening this gift again and again, as many times as you need.

MY DEPRESSION SCALE

Use the handout My Depression Scale to help children identify where they are with their symptoms. This scale can help children communicate to you about their symptoms and whether their symptoms have recently improved or regressed.

My Depression Scale

1 → I feel good! I'm enjoying life. I have things I'm looking forward to. I'm getting things done that need to get done. I'm doing okay (or well) in school, or in my job. I have at least one good friend.

2 → I'm not sure if I'm starting to feel any symptoms or not. It seems like things are going okay though!

3 → I'm starting to get tired and/or frustrated more easily. It's getting harder to motivate myself to get things done. However, I'm still keeping up with all of my responsibilities.

4 → I'm tired. Everything I do takes so much effort. I'm getting some things done when I have the energy, but I'm falling behind in my responsibilities. I just want to hide in bed and avoid everyone and everything.

5 → I'm not getting out of bed on my own. I'm not showering. I don't care about anything. My friends and family would be better off without me. I feel like there's nothing to look forward to and that I'll never feel happy.

An accompanying story

The Troll and the Snail

Once upon a time, in a village far away, there was a troll called William who lived under a dark and gloomy bridge. Most of the village trolls lived in cottages in the sunny part of town, but not William. William lived where he had cold, wet cobblestones for walls, thick, earthy mud for floors, and the constant drippy-drip-drip that came from the stalactites on the underside of the bridge. William didn't understand why he preferred the dark and gloomy space under the bridge—it seemed like all the other trolls actually liked sunny, bright spaces. He also didn't understand why he preferred to be left alone when all the other trolls liked to be with others. And he certainly didn't understand why all the other trolls were so cheerful (he could hear their laughter and joyful conversations as they passed over the bridge). All William seemed to feel was nothing, dread, or just really sad, hopeless feelings. William just wasn't like the other trolls at all.

Well, one day a snail came to live under the bridge. William was not so sure about sharing his space with the snail. Especially *this* snail. *This* snail had a painted shell—a shell full of brightly colored rainbows, flowers, and ladybugs. And when the snail was unpacking his belongings, William noticed a tambourine, jellybeans, and crayons in the snail's backpack. "I'm not so sure how this is going to work out," William thought to himself. William preferred the quiet and gloom. The snail seemed to prefer music and joy.

But as time passed by, William and the snail became friends. The snail shared his jellybeans with William—something William had never tried before. And William liked them!

The snail played his tambourine at bedtime and William started to sleep a little better. He even found the security of his friend's company and music to be soothing and comforting.

William and the snail started spending afternoons decorating the underside of the bridge with pictures, doodles, silly words that made them giggle, and big, puffy rainbows. Once in a while this actually made William feel joyful and amused. Other days they would play cards and make paper boats to float down the river.

William noticed that little by little he was feeling less gloom and more joy. It was a strange but wonderful feeling to feel joy! He started to feel less comfortable with gloomy things and more comfortable with happy things—he was starting to feel more like the other trolls.

He said "Thank you" to his friend for helping him feel better. "I never knew sunshine and music and jellybeans and playing would be so much fun!"

Sometimes William would feel the gloom start to creep back, but he remembered that if he stayed close to friends, kept busy, and didn't hide from everyone, then others could help him keep the gloom away.

An activity to go along with the story

COLOR A SNAIL SHELL

The snail in the story enjoys many things such as his tambourine, jellybeans, and crayons. Draw or write some of the things that you enjoy on the snail's shell on the following coloring page.

 ## Affirmations

✓ I feel gratitude.

✓ This sadness is temporary.

✓ There is joy and hope, even when I cannot feel it.

*

Decorate the snail's shell with things that make you smile or make you feel happy. Use words and/or pictures!

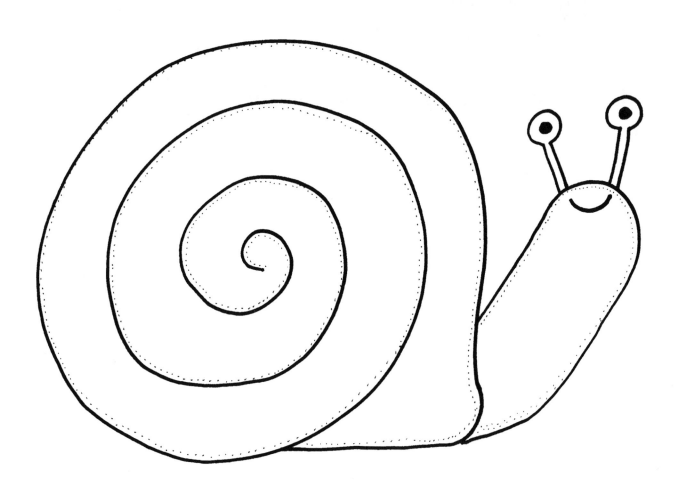

CHAPTER 10

Increasing Self-confidence and Self-esteem

. . . .

Challenges

The child has low self-esteem.

The child doesn't recognize their strengths.

Goal

The child will feel good about themself and be able to recognize their strengths.

Skills: Increasing self-confidence and self-esteem

The skills addressed in this chapter include recognizing personal strengths and talents, receiving and reflecting on positive feedback, finding new ways to express and define the self, recognizing accomplishments, and practicing affirmations.

✚ Interventions

A BOOK ABOUT ME

Journaling is a wonderful medium for kids of all ages to express who they are and what they feel passionate about. Encourage children to keep a journal in which they can write and draw whatever they wish. For those who have difficulty thinking of what to write or draw, refer to the handout Creative Prompts for Journaling.

POWER STONES

Keep a bowl of Power Stones in your counseling office or on a shelf for clients to look at and hold. They are great conversation starters! Or make these with clients so they can use them on their own for inspiration, mantras, reminders, or affirmation. The stones have inspiring words and phrases on them.

Materials

- Words or phrases cut from magazines that invoke a sense of self-confidence (e.g. Power, Confidence, I can, Strength, Courage, Unstoppable, etc.)

- Scissors

- Decoupage glue

- Smooth flat stones

- Small paintbrush

Directions

- Cut the phrases and words out of the magazines.

- Apply a thin layer of decoupage glue to the underside of the word or phrase.

- Place the phrase or word onto a stone.

- Use the paintbrush to apply a thin layer of decoupage glue over the paper. Press down lightly to seal the paper and smooth out any bubbles.

- Allow the Power Stones to dry thoroughly.

Variation

If you do not have magazines, you can also purchase scrapbook paper that has similar words on it; or use your most creative handwriting to write your own onto strips of plain paper. Alternatively, use acrylic paint to write your own words and phrases onto the rocks.

Creative Prompts for Journaling

- Draw yourself as: a playing card; a type of candy; a flower; a tree; an animal; a cartoon character; a superhero; a house; a quilt.

- Make a list of words, quotes, and phrases that inspire you.

- Draw yourself in a rainstorm. Use your smallest handwriting to write your greatest worries in lines of rain falling down on you.

- Draw yourself in the center of a page. Draw a protective barrier around yourself. Draw the things that you feel you need protection from on the outside of the barrier.

- Use graphic novel or comic strip format to show what a typical day is like for you.

- Make a collage and/or sketch pictures of a dream vacation destination.

- Draw a picture of a place—real or imagined—where you feel safe and relaxed.

- Write the lyrics to one of your favorite songs and highlight the words that you relate to the most.

- What would an ideal day look like to you? Describe it.

- Draw a map of your heart. Fill it in with roads, pictures, or words that indicate what you are passionate about and what you love. Are there parts of the heart that are broken? Are there parts that are healing?

- Reflect on what you need in order to get your day started right. What would that look like?

- Draw a family portrait. Draw each family member as an animal, a plant, or a character.

- Describe your favorite meal.

- Draw a sinking ship. Who is on it?

*

- If you drive or ride to a place frequently (e.g. work or school), list the landmarks or other things you see on that drive that catch your attention (e.g. the red shed, a broken window, the crooked tree, the odd-shaped building, etc.).

- Draw or write about a recurring dream or nightmare you have. What do you think it means?

- Describe a time that an animal had a positive effect on your life.

- Draw your current bedroom or the bedroom you wish you had.

- List or draw your favorite toys from childhood.

- Cut out a picture from a magazine and glue it into your journal. Alter the picture in some way (e.g. draw over a part of it).

- Draw a timeline of all of the places you have lived—include apartments, houses, shelters, cars, campers, etc.

- What are the best and worst moments of the day?

- Write about a friend from earlier in your life. What do you think you learned from that friend? What do you think that friend learned from you?

- Cut out pieces of paper from a magazine with colors, patterns, or words you like. Glue them onto your journal page.

- Write a letter to your future self.

- Write a letter to your younger self.

- Glue colorful or decorated envelopes onto pages in your journal. You can store letters, memorabilia, or things you've written, in the envelopes. It's like a secret hiding spot in your journal.

- Fill an entire journal page with things you are grateful for.

- Create a list of the things that bring you comfort.

- Describe the perfect wardrobe for you—pretend that money is not a barrier and you can fill your closet with whatever you like. You can also draw this or cut images from a catalogue and glue them onto the page.

- Write the word COURAGE on a page. List the times you were courageous on the page. Do the same for other words such as ANGER, SCARED, SHY, SMART, RUDE, etc.

- List five things you want to accomplish in your life.

- Vent—just let it all out. Write everything you wish you could say about a person or situation and just go for it!

- If you could spend your day as someone else, who would you be for the day? Why?

- Fold the corners of a journal page any way you like. Decorate and write on and around the shape of the folds.

- Draw the same shape, symbol, letter, or number all over the page and then color it in.

- Write a word in bubble or block letters and fill in the letters with different patterns.

- Cut a rectangle from a piece of paper and then decorate it like a door (any design you like!). Tape one side of the door onto a journal page so that you can open and shut it like a door. Draw something behind the door. Is it something you want to see at the door? Is it a monster or something scary in your closet? Is it a door that opens to a magical land?

- Who is someone you feel sad for? Why?

- Draw a small circle. Then draw concentric circles equal to as many years old you are. Does it look like a tree that's been cut? Pretend each ring represents a year of your life (just like a tree!) and write something in each circle that happened that year for you.

- Write a rap or a poem about something that annoys you.

- Trace your hand onto a page in your journal. Fill the hand with doodles of your favorite things.

- Pretend you have $100 to donate to anyone or any organization that is not related to you. Who would you give it to?

POWER PEG DOLL NECKLACES

Younger children often love these necklaces for a few reasons—making them is enjoyable, the dolls can be played with or worn, and the dolls serve as a reminder of the child's strengths. I start the activity by asking the child: "What are your personal strengths that help you to get through tough situations?" You can refer to the handout titled Personal Strengths List for ideas. The child can identify as many strengths as they like. Next, follow these directions to make the Power Peg Doll Necklace.

Materials

- Paper (decorative or plain)

- Thin-tipped permanent ink pen

- Small-tipped paintbrushes

- Wooden peg dolls (blank, unpainted ones)

- Acrylic paints or colored pencils for adding facial features and hair

- String or ribbon

- Glue

- Eye screws

Directions

- Choose one of the child's strengths and write it on a thin strip of paper— use the permanent ink pen for this. Set the paper strip aside.

- Paint or draw the doll's facial features. Allow to dry if using paint.

- Add hair using string or ribbon and glue. You can also draw or paint the hair.

- Apply a thin layer of glue to the strip of paper that says the child's strength and apply it to the doll. Some kids will want their "strength" glued under the doll's clothing to keep it hidden or private; others will want it to show. Either way is fine.

- Use paper or paint to create clothing for the doll. Paper can be wrapped around the doll for clothing.

- Screw the eye screw into the top of the doll's head.

- Slip a ribbon or string through the eye screw hole. Adjust the length of the necklace so the child can pull it on and off over their head. Tie a knot where needed.

Note: Blank, unpainted wooden peg dolls can be purchased at craft supply shops—usually in the wooden aisle section. If you are buying several at a time it can be more cost-effective to buy them online in bulk. Use your online search engine to find "blank wooden peg doll."

*

Personal Strengths List

- Active
- Adventurous
- Affectionate
- Agile
- Ambitious
- Appreciative
- Athletic
- Brave
- Brilliant
- Calm
- Candid
- Capable
- Carefree
- Caring
- Cautious
- Charming
- Clever
- Compassionate
- Concerned
- Confident

- Conscientious
- Considerate
- Cooperative
- Courageous
- Creative
- Curious
- Daring
- Decisive
- Dependable
- Determined
- Devoted
- Disciplined
- Eager
- Easy-going
- Efficient
- Energetic
- Enthusiastic
- Ethical
- Fair
- Faithful

- Fearless
- Focused
- Forgiving
- Friendly
- Funny
- Generous
- Gentle
- Good friend
- Good listener
- Grateful
- Hardworking
- Helpful
- Honest
- Hopeful
- Humble
- Humorous
- Imaginative
- Independent
- Innovative
- Inquisitive

- Intelligent
- Joyful
- Kind
- Logical
- Lovable
- Loving
- Loyal
- Lucky
- Mature
- Modest
- Non-judging
- Obedient
- Observant
- Open-minded
- Optimistic
- Organized
- Passionate
- Patient
- Peaceful

- Perceptive
- Persistent
- Persuasive
- Pleasant
- Polite
- Protective
- Proud
- Quick
- Quiet
- Rational
- Realistic
- Reliable
- Respectful
- Responsible
- Self-reliant
- Self-respecting
- Sensitive
- Silly
- Sincere

- Skillful
- Smart
- Sociable
- Strong
- Studious
- Supportive
- Sweet
- Talented
- Thoughtful
- Tolerant
- Tough
- Trusting
- Trustworthy
- Understanding
- Unpretentious
- Versatile
- Warm-hearted
- Wise
- Witty

SUPERHEROES

Superheroes are figurines made with old-fashioned wooden clothespins and represent varying superhero powers. The superhero powers are based on the personal strengths that the child already possesses. This activity helps children identify and celebrate their own personal strengths, and to look at themselves as having their own unique superpowers.

Materials

- Old-fashioned wooden clothespins (found in crafts stores—any size is fine)

- Permanent markers in a variety of colors

- Paper (optional)

- Glue

- Embroidery string in a variety of colors (for hair)

- Scissors

- Scrap pieces of thin cloth

Directions

- Have a discussion about what the child's personal strengths are. Refer to the Superpowers symbols handout if needed to help the child identify their personal strengths.

- If the child is making one figurine then have them choose their No. I favorite or strongest personal strength; if making two, then choose two, and so on.

- Choose a symbol to represent that personal strength, or "superpower." Refer to the handout if you need ideas for symbols.

- Draw a face on the clothespin using permanent markers.

- Next, draw the symbol onto the body of the figurine. You can also draw the symbol on paper and cut it out and glue it on (this is especially helpful if the child makes a mistake and wants to start over—you can glue a paper symbol on instead).

- Color around the symbol. The child can add superhero attire and accessories, including a bodysuit, tights, and boots.

- Create the hero's hair. It is easiest to trim pieces of hair to the same length and then use a separate piece of string to tie around the hair in the middle.

The middle part, where the knot is, is then tied to the head of the figurine. For short hair, trim it to length.

- Finally, if the child wants a cape, you can make one from cloth. Cut a scrap piece of cloth into a "T" shape. The top extensions from the "T" are tied around the superhero's neck. Trim to size and shape as necessary.

- When the figurines are completed, allow the glue and ink to dry. Children can use these figurines in imaginative play, as reminders of their own personal strengths, and/or they can display them somewhere that the child can be reminded each day that they have strengths and power to get through challenging moments.

JAR OF STARS

A Jar of Stars is an activity that takes preparation and time, but is well worth it. The end result is a jar that has been decorated and filled with positive messages written by people who know the child. Family members, school staff, members of the child's athletic team or clubs, and community members can participate by writing one or more messages. When the child is experiencing a dip in their self-esteem, the Jar of Stars is there to remind them of all the people who love and care about them and/or admire their talents and strengths.

Whether you are a parental figure or a care provider/counselor, your role in this activity is to coordinate and contact the child's loved ones to see if they will help. You can use the handout Jar of Stars as a template for the messages. The easiest and quickest way to gather the messages is to ask for them via email or social media (but privately). That way, you can write the messages on the stars for the child. However, if you have frequent contact with any of the child's family or community you can directly ask them to complete a message for the child.

Next, decorate a jar with a lid. If nothing else, tie a pretty ribbon around the lid, or put some stickers on it. Fill the jar with the messages and give it to the child.

Note: Keep a separate record of the messages just in case the child loses the jar.

TODAY I WILL BE...

Today I Will Be… is a sign you hang somewhere in your home or office. The top says "Today I will be…" and the bottom has strips of paper with various adjectives and phrases on them that are meant to be positive and encouraging. For example, "Today I will be…kind/brave/a good friend to someone." A person who comes across the sign is encouraged to tear off one of the words or phrases as a reminder to create a positive moment or mood.

You can create your own sign or you can use the sign included with this book. Use scissors to trim the lines between each word so that someone can tear the word off as needed.

ALTERNATIVE SELF-PORTRAITS

There are endless ways for children to create self-portraits using various themes, but oftentimes kids are introduced to doing portraits in traditional style (i.e. drawing a picture of themselves using accurate physical details of their face and body). If a child does not like how they look and/or if they do not like how they make themself look in the portrait, the result can be a child who feels bad about themself.

This activity provides *alternative* ways to create self-portraits so that the child feels validated and good about themself when the "portrait" is complete. These portraits are meant to be fun and expressive. Here are some examples of ways to do so.

Metaphorical/Symbolic Self-Portrait

The child chooses a symbol or metaphor for themself and creates a portrait of it. They can add their name or an image of themself within the portrait if they like, but the focus of the portrait is the metaphor or symbol. Examples include a mountain lion, a princess, a warrior, a butterfly, or a phoenix.

Cartography Self-Portrait

The child draws a self-portrait using a map as a metaphor for themself. The entire map represents who they are. They can even draw the map as an outline of their face or body if they wish, but again, the focus is on the overall metaphor of the land representing the child as a whole. Here is an example "legend" you can use in this activity but the child can create their own.

- Bodies of water: Hopes, dreams, wishes.

- Forests: Passions, hobbies, interests, talents, personal strengths. The child can make individual trees and label each tree with these if they like.

- Treacherous landmarks: Traumatic events and/or experiences in which the child was hurt physically or emotionally. Here are some examples: Shark-infested waters might represent unsafe people; quicksand might represent experiences in which the child felt they had no control; hostile territory could be places where the child felt like they and/or their family were treated unfairly or where they felt unsafe; a desert could represent a time the child felt thirsty for more in their life but did not have the resources to get out; a prison could represent a time the child felt imprisoned by something or someone.

- Helping landmarks: Places and people who helped the child overcome challenges. A bridge could represent someone who helped them get out of a bad situation or helped them achieve something; a lighthouse could be someone who helped them with a significant event; a sanctuary could be a place where they felt safe.

- A cemetery: Things the child misses or grieves. They could draw gravestones for each major loss in their life, from pets, people, and objects to things such as trust.

- Mountains/mountain ranges: Challenges, difficulties, things that are hard to overcome.

Self-Portrait Collage

Allow plenty of time for the child to gather the materials required for this project. In essence, the child collects the following and then glues them onto a poster board: quotes, images, song lyrics, and words that the child relates to or that resonate with them. These can be cut from magazines, printed out from a website, or copied in the child's handwriting or artwork. The child can also add fortunes from a cookie, a wrapper or label from their favorite food, a special note or card from someone, or other paper items. Once the child has a variety and number of collage items, choose a poster-sized piece of paper and arrange the items on it. Once the child feels good about the arrangement, glue them into place.

Calm; relaxed; "goes with the flow"

Protective

Resilient; bounces back from tough situations

Hard worker; persistent

Organized; detail oriented   III   1, 2, 3

Gracious; thankful

Peaceful; forgiving

Strong; reliable; dependable

Balanced; fair

Adaptable

Inquisitive; problem solver

Flexible

Friendly

Good at many things; multi-tasks well

Helpful; kind; generous

Passionate; energetic   E

Patient

Listens well to others

Humble

Sees the good in others

Artistic; musical; talented

Intuitive

Sympathetic; empathic

Loving; nurturing; caring   XO

Superpowers and their symbols

Learns things quickly; smart; has great ideas 💡

Cautious; careful; vigilant ⊘ ▽ 👁

Leader; collaborative; team player ⟷ ᴜ

Predictable; reliable; responsible ☀/☾ ⇨

Humorous; funny; cheers people up ☺ LOL HA ○

Resourceful; finds new ways to get things done 👓 🔍 📖

Playful; relaxed ▷

Optimistic; hopeful; encouraging ☀ ✚ ⊞

Brave; courageous 🛡

Loyal; devoted ⋈ ∞

Integrity; honest ⬟

Good boundaries with others 🛑 ⊘

ADD YOUR OWN HERE:

Super powers and their symbols

A JAR OF STARS

A "Jar of Stars" is a great gift for anyone needing a smile, a mood lifter, or a reminder of how important they are.

I am putting together a "Jar of Stars" for this person:

_____

Please fill out one or more "stars" below and return it to me by this date: _____. You can mail the star/s to this address if needed: _____.

I will collect "stars" from participants and put them in a decorated jar for the person noted above.

☆ Something I appreciate about you:

_____
_____
_____

From: _____

☆ I've noticed this amazing thing about you:

_____
_____
_____

From: _____

☆ I enjoy this about you:

_____
_____
_____

From: _____

Today
I will be......

BRAVE

Patient

A good friend

Generous

Amazing! I'm amazing every day!

Someone's hero

nice to someone who could use some kindness

Creative

Today
I will be....

BADGES

Badges are a way to encourage a younger child to set goals and earn badges for meeting those goals. Badges can be created and designed to meet the individual needs of the child. They do not need to be elaborate—they can be as simple as adding a symbol or word to a small circle or other shape on paper.

Materials

- Paper
- Scissors
- Colored pens/markers

Directions

- Create a small list of goals that the child is working on. Make sure the goals are achievable because the purpose of earning these badges is to help the child feel success and therefore boost their self-esteem and confidence.

- Decide on a place to display the badges once the child earns them. A simple idea is to put them on a larger piece of paper or poster board. The child can decorate the poster if they like. Another idea is to create a book or passport-style booklet where the child earns a badge on each page.

- Make the badges. You can design the badges to be various shapes, or stick to one shape. You can download shape outlines from the internet or you can draw your own. There are also various stencils and objects you can trace around (e.g. sometimes I will use the bottom of a small glass for making circle shapes).

- Put a picture or words on the badges to show what the badge was earned for.

- Decorate the badges or have the child decorate them.

- As the child achieves their various goals, they earn the indicated badges. They can then collect them on their poster or book (or whatever medium you chose).

AFFIRMATIONS

There are many affirmations noted in this book, but here I've included a handout listing additional ones. Affirmations are positive messages we tell ourselves. The more you use affirmations, the more your brain believes them. So, pick an affirmation each day or week and try it!

Affirmations

- I can do this.

- Let it go.

- I can do whatever I put my mind to.

- I believe in myself.

- I make healthy choices.

- I am in control of my body.

- I can quiet my thoughts.

- I will look for the good in today.

- It's okay to make mistakes.

- I accept who I am even when I make mistakes.

- I will be kind to others and myself today.

- Today I will give my best in everything I do.

- I am open-minded.

- I am beautiful.

- I am handsome.

- I have people in my life who care about me and love me.

- I can try new things.

- I am getting better.

- I listen to my heart.

- I'm deserving of love and kindness.

*

- Some days are easier than others.

- I am in charge of my feelings.

- I can learn from my mistakes.

- I find inspiration in each day.

- This world needs me.

- I have many talents.

- I am loved.

- I am grateful.

- I am a great kid.

- I'm a smart kid—I can do this.

- I will take a deep breath.

- I can think for myself.

- I love my body.

- I show others how I want to be treated.

- I am full of love and light.

- I matter.

- I can listen to my intuition ("gut feelings").

- No one is perfect—each of us is doing the best we can.

- I have a loving heart.

- I am not alone.

- I am a good kid.

An accompanying story
The Teeny Tiny Wizard

Once upon a time there was a powerful wizard. The wizard was so powerful that he could change the weather, he could make things disappear, and he could even talk to animals. But as powerful as this wizard was, there was one thing he could not do—he could not change his size.

You see, the wizard was the size of a cricket. He was very teeny tiny. And because of his size, it was difficult for people to even know if he was around. This made the wizard feel very shy and unsure of himself.

One day the Teeny Tiny Wizard was studying a speck of dust when a beetle came by. The wizard, if you remember, could talk to animals. "Good afternoon, lovely beetle," said the wizard. The beetle grunted at the wizard and kept going. "Did I offend you, Beetle? I didn't mean to offend! I just meant to say hello on this beautiful day."

The beetle turned around and grumpily spoke: "It is not a beautiful day, it is a horrible day! I lost my favorite bow tie and now I am sad and angry and feeling quite blue."

The wizard's face lit up and he cheerily replied: "Well luckily for you I can help! I have all sorts of powers and I will help you find your bow tie!"

The beetle looked once more at the wizard. He wanted to believe that the wizard could help him, but how could something so small help him find his bow tie?

"Come, come—over here!" the wizard said. The beetle followed the wizard over to a red and white spotted mushroom. Leaning against the mushroom was a beautiful staff. The wizard picked up the staff and pointed it at the ground. A swirl of mist appeared in the same spot where the staff had pointed. The wizard then peered into the mist. By now the beetle was curious, but still doubtful that the wizard could help him.

"Hmmmmmmmm," said the wizard.

"Uh-huh," said the wizard.

"Oh! Oh Oh!" said the wizard.

And then the wizard started laughing. "I know where your bow tie is, Beetle! And I'm sorry to laugh but it really is quite funny! Your bow tie, Beetle, is on you! You are wearing it! But you can't see it because it slipped to the back of your neck where you can't see it!"

The beetle felt around his neck and, yes indeed, he felt the band of his bow tie around his neck. He pulled the band around until the bow was in front. The beetle laughed with the wizard: "Oh dear wizard, I feel like a fool! I was wearing it the whole time! How can I repay you for helping me and taking up your time?"

"Well, you already gave me something," the wizard replied. "You gave me a reminder that I really am helpful even if I am very small. And I thank you for that."

From that day forward, the Teeny Tiny Wizard and the beetle became good friends. The beetle, who travelled on the ground and in the air, told all of his friends about the Teeny Tiny Wizard, and soon everybody in the area knew that the wizard existed and that he was a very helpful friend indeed.

 ## An activity to go along with the story

MAKE A WAND

For this activity I use sticks, paint, washi tape, and ribbons to make magic wands. Sticks can be painted with lines or dots, or in sections of color. Washi tape can be added for stripes and decorative patterns. Ribbons can be tied to the wand for decoration as well.

While you make a wand with the child, talk about a time the child felt confident or successful in doing something.

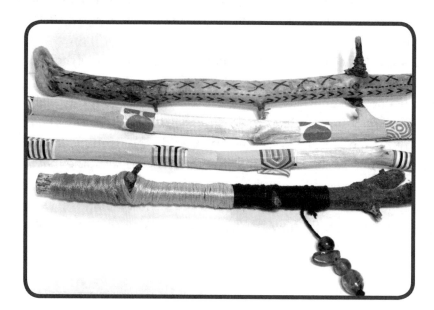

 ## Affirmations

✓ I am good at many things.

✓ No matter my age and size, I can do powerful things.

CHAPTER 11

Loss and Grief

. . . .

! Challenges

The child is grieving the loss of a loved one, pet, place, or thing.

The child is having trouble adjusting to a change.

◎ Goals

The child will have some added skills and resources to cope with their grief.

The child will have new coping strategies to help them manage this new change in their life.

✱ Skills: Coping with grief and loss

The skills in this chapter address remembering and honoring the loved one, sharing feelings and memories about the loved one, saying goodbye, and/or providing some closure around the loss.

✚ Interventions

ALTERED SCRABBLE BOARD

The Altered Scrabble Board is a visual way to share and show memories about a person, place, or pet the child misses. When completed, it can be hung on a wall or added to a Remembrance Table (see page 194).

Materials

- A Scrabble® board game that is no longer being used

- White glue

- Recycled piece of cardboard that will fit on the back of the board

- Scissors

- Clippings, ephemera, and photos of the place, person, or pet being remembered

- Hanger (optional)

Directions

- Help the child make a list of words that remind them of the person, place, or pet.

- Prioritize the words that the child ends up relating to most, or liking the most.

- Flip the Scrabble board over and glue a large piece of recycled cardboard to the back of it—this will stabilize the board so that it won't fold or bend anymore.

- Use the Scrabble tiles to create as many of the child's words that you can on the board, connecting them to each other in crossword format—the words can intersect each other.

- Once the words have been arranged, glue them in place.

- Glue any photos or memorabilia to the board, in and around the words.

- If you'd like to hang the board, attach a hanger to the back.

MEMORY LANTERNS

Memory Lanterns are battery operated candles that have been wrapped in tracing paper decorated with words and pictures about a loved one. There are many ways to use Memory Lanterns—here are some suggestions:

- Light the candle on special occasions or celebrations when the person, place, or pet will be especially missed. For example, light the candle during a family gathering in memory of a person who used to attend—this is a way to still include them in your celebration as well as to remember them.

- Add the lantern to an altar or Remembrance Table (see next activity).

- Light the candle during the funeral or other ceremony regarding the loss.

- Light the candle when you miss that person, place, or pet.

Materials

- Tracing paper

- A large battery-operated candle with a smooth and clear glass holder

- Scissors

- Permanent ink markers, crayons, and/or coloring pencils

- Tape or string

Directions

Wrap a piece of tracing paper around the candle holder. Mark the height and width of the paper for the holder and then trim the paper down to the size needed. You will want the strip of paper to wrap the entire way around your candle holder. Use decorative trim scissors if you want a patterned border along the top and/or bottom of your candle holder.

Have the child draw and decorate a picture of the person, place, or pet they miss on the strip of tracing paper. They can also add symbols, words, quotes, or stories of their favorite memories. The supervising adult can help with any of the drawings or words if necessary.

Wrap the finished drawing around the candle holder. Tie a piece of string around the picture or tape the picture in place.

REMEMBRANCE TABLES AND ALTARS

Create a small table or area in the home where you can honor the person or pet that has passed away. It can be as large or small as needed. The area is used to display photos, memorabilia, candles, Memory Lanterns, Memory Jars, quotes, and other items that honor your loved one and your grief.

FUNERAL SCRIPTS FOR PETS

When a pet dies, some families hold funerals and others do not. A funeral can be a positive experience for the child for many reasons:

- It gathers loved ones together, which in and of itself can be supportive for the child.

- It provides an opportunity to share feelings and memories about the pet.

- It provides a way to honor the pet and say goodbye, especially if the child has not had the chance to do so yet.

- It provides real-life experience in dealing with death.

A "funeral" can be as simple as standing around the toilet and saying a few words before flushing a dead pet goldfish. It can be as elaborate as inviting friends and family together to share memories of a beloved dog and then scattering its ashes in a special place.

Funeral scripts (see handout) can be helpful for parents and care providers. They provide an outline of quick and simple words to say in child-friendly language.

Funeral Scripts for Pets

Script 1

I/We will miss you, _____. You were, and always will be, loved.

Script 2

My favorite memory about _____ was the time

_____

_____

_____

_____

_____

(tell your favorite memory). I love this memory because it describes _____
so well. I will also miss the way _____
(describe some personality traits or habits of the pet, e.g. "I will also miss the way
Peanut would go sledding with us in winter"). It is a very sad time for us to say goodbye
to you, _____. You will always be loved and missed.

Script 3

Today we have gathered together to say goodbye to a beloved family member and pet,
_____.

_____ was like other (name the animal, e.g. dogs) in that he was

_____

_____

_____

(name the characteristics that are common to that animal, i.e. loyal, funny, affectionate).

✱

But he was also unique and special to us in particular because he _____

_____

_____.

(describe the things that made your pet unique compared to other pets like him). We thank him for everything he shared with us, including _____

_____

_____.

(insert any characteristics and moments you are most grateful for). We are heartbroken and sad to say goodbye to _____. Rest in peace, _____. We love and miss you so very much.

SPIRIT THEATER

Note: A Spirit Theater will, most likely, be more helpful for counselors who work with children, but parents/guardians can determine if this activity meets the needs of their own child/ren.

A Spirit Theater is a decorated cardboard box (shoebox size) that has figurines and objects related to death inside it. The figurines can be chosen, moved about, and rearranged for expressive play regarding death. If you are a counselor who works with children, add a variety of pieces including as many cross-cultural components as is feasible. Figurines and objects might include (but are not limited to):

- angels
- wings
- caskets
- gravestones
- bridge
- religious figureheads, such as a priest or rabbi
- spiritual figureheads, such as a shaman
- religious or spiritual places (e.g. a church)
- funeral pyre
- skeleton
- grim reaper
- skull
- clock
- hourglass
- candle
- sundial
- mummy
- wheel
- shovel
- various weapons
- hearse
- hospital or medical facility
- ambulance
- bones
- metaphorical pieces such as a phoenix, rainbow, or a butterfly
- labyrinth
- pyramid
- crystals and gems
- religious objects.

During a counseling session the child can explore the pieces and then create a picture with ones of their choosing. This provides an opportunity for the child to express themself using the figurines, as well as to tell the counselor about the picture they have created. The Spirit Theater can be separate from your collection of sand tray items (if you use a sand tray) or added to an existing collection.

If you are a parent, you could collect objects and figurines as they relate to your own family and culture. The child could be given the opportunity to explore the items and even play with them. Many times, parents feel uncomfortable discussing death with their children for a host of reasons. However, death is a normal part of the life cycle and children often want to know more about it. Play is an age-appropriate means for exploring the concept of death.

PAPER ANGELS

Not all religions, cultures, or families believe in angels, but if you have a child in your life who does, this activity is quick and easy to do with them. Use the angel template provided and follow the directions. The child can decorate the angel in the likeness of the loved one who has died, if that is desired. They can also add a pipe cleaner halo. The angel can be added to a Remembrance Table (page 194), dresser, or windowsill in memory of the person.

Make an angel

- Color and decorate the angel below (color both sides!)
- cut the angel out
- trim along the dotted lines - - - - - - - -
- fold the wings back and slide one wing into the other where the dotted lines were
- tape the wings down where they connect along the bottom

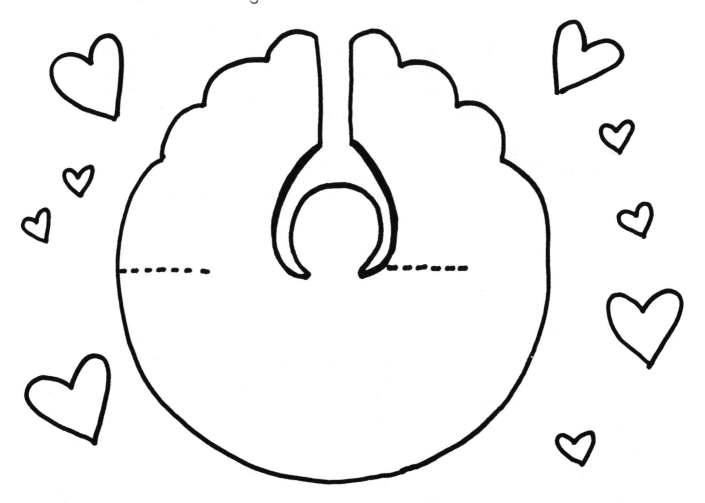

WHAT WAS LEFT UNSAID

There are times when a loved one dies before the child has had a chance for closure or to say what they wanted and needed to say to the person. There are also times when a loved one dies when the child is too young to know all of the details of the death (e.g. if the death was a suicide or an overdose), or even to understand much about death itself (e.g. if the child was two years old when the person died). In these situations it can be helpful to provide an opportunity for the child to express what's been left unsaid and unexpressed about the loved one's death. This can help the child have some closure by having the opportunity to say what they need to. Here are a couple of ways to provide the opportunity:

- Decorate an envelope with the words "What was left unsaid." The child can write down (or draw) whatever they want and need to say to the loved one and put it in the envelope. The envelope could be added to a Remembrance Table (see page 194); it could be added to an Altered Scrabble Board (see page 192); it could be left open so the child can add more to it at a later time; it could be sealed after the child has expressed what they wanted to say; or it could be added to another piece of artwork (older youth can create a piece of art in which their envelope and contents become part of the art piece).

- You can also provide a small journal for the child, titled "What was left unsaid." The journal works well for kids who are old enough to write or draw and who might need more time to express their thoughts and feelings over a period of time. The journal can be an open-ended means for the child to say what they want to, or about, the loved one who has died.

MEMORY JARS

A Memory Jar is a clear glass jar that is filled with mementoes about the loved one who has died. The jars can be comforting to make and then look through when you or the child is missing that loved one.

If you want to add a "label" for the jar, you can cut a strip of paper that reaches around the jar, decorate it with the loved one's name and pictures, and then tape or tie the label in place.

Examples of items that might go in a Memory Jar are:

- photographs (e.g. of the loved person or pet, of places the child enjoyed going with the loved one, of family holidays or celebrations the loved one was part of, etc.)

- an obituary

- any mementoes from the funeral or memorial service (e.g. prayers or poems said during the service or ceremony)

- trinkets that remind you of the loved one or that belonged to the loved one

- stories about favorite memories of the loved one (these can be written on strips of paper and then rolled and tied into scrolls to fit in the jar)

- something that shows the loved one's handwriting (e.g. a birthday card or postcard the loved one gave the child).

REMEMBRANCE ACTIVITIES

Remembrance activities are those that commemorate, celebrate, and honor the memory of a person, pet, or other loss (e.g. a house lost in a fire). There are several ways to do so, but I will highlight a few of my favorites.

Remembrance Flags

Materials

- Plain fabric such as cotton, muslin cloth, or canvas

- Fabric markers (make sure to choose markers with colors that will show up on your fabric—if you are using darker-colored fabric, purchase white fabric pens; if you are using light-colored fabrics, purchase darker fabric pens)

- Scissors

- Ribbon or twine

Directions

- Cut the fabric into similar sized rectangles.

- Decorate the rectangles with memories, pictures, prayers, wishes, or hopes related to the person, animal, loss, or event.

- Cut small holes along the top of the rectangles so that ribbon or twine can be woven through the flags. Attach all the flags in this manner to make a garland.

- Display or hang the garland.

Chinese Fire Lanterns

Chinese Fire Lanterns can be purchased online, either in bulk (for a large event) or individually (for a solitary event). Many people use these lanterns to release during a remembrance ceremony or ritual. After memories are shared, loved ones prepare their lanterns and release them at the same time in honor of the mourned loved one.

Chinese Fire Lanterns are a beautiful tradition, but there are challenges to using them—they are fragile (order more than you need because they tear easily), they are weather dependent (you can't release them in stormy or inclement weather), and they can impact the environment and/or local habitats (check your local rules, regulations, and resources accordingly).

Remembrance Candle

After the loss of a family member, holidays and family gatherings can be especially challenging for a child. A Remembrance Candle is lit by the child (or family) to encapsulate the presence of the family member no longer with them. When special occasions and gatherings occur, the child can bring the candle out and light it. In this way, the candle holds the space and honor for the person who has passed. It also gives the child a way to still include their loved one in family traditions. For younger children a battery-operated candle is recommended.

An accompanying story
The Girl Who Lost Her Shadow

Minuit was a girl who loved her shadow. She played with her shadow every day and the shadow went everywhere she went.

But one day, Minuit woke up and noticed something was missing. Her shadow was no longer with her. She hunted everywhere for her shadow but could not find it. Minuit then asked the adults: "Where is my shadow?" And the adults gave her a very sad look and said: "We are so sorry, Minuit, but your shadow has gone—you won't see your shadow again."

"Of course I will!" said Minuit. "My shadow is just lost somewhere! It would never leave me, I just know it."

And Minuit went off again to look for her shadow.

After many hours Minuit still could not find her shadow. She had looked everywhere. She had asked everyone. Minuit was exhausted and heartbroken. She finally realized that her shadow truly was gone.

Minuit stomped her feet and clenched her fists. She let out loud angry sobs. "How could my shadow leave me?! How?!" Minuit was so very distraught with anger. It wasn't fair that her shadow was gone. How could her shadow do this to her?

Minuit wiped her tears and wondered if she could have done anything different to prevent her shadow leaving her. Could she have stopped it leaving so soon?

Minuit curled up in her favorite cozy spot and felt sad. Deeply sad. She closed her eyes and remembered all the good times she had with her shadow and she knew she was going to miss it for a very long time—probably forever.

But then Minuit decided she needed to give her shadow a proper goodbye because she had loved it so very much and had shared so many memories with it. She sat down and made a card for her shadow as a way to say goodbye. She drew beautiful hearts all over the card and wrote in big puffy letters: "I will miss you forever, Shadow. I love you." She hung the card on her wall. Sometimes she looked at the card and felt sad because she missed her shadow very much. But sometimes she smiled, too, because she remembered all the good times they had together.

 ## An activity to go along with the story

STAINED GLASS HEART

The Stained Glass Heart is a metaphor for grief. When a loved one dies, your heart might feel shattered. But over time you will find ways for the light to shine through your heart again. Talk about this metaphor as the child colors the Stained Glass Heart.

 ## Affirmations

✓ Love lasts forever.

✓ I am thankful for the time I shared with _____.

✓ It's okay for me to grieve.

*

"STAINED GLASS" HEART

1. Cut the heart from the paper.
2. Cut the white sections out (poke your scissors into the center of each section and trim carefully).
3. Cut pieces of colored cellophane or tissue paper to fit into the sections. Glue them into place. These pieces create the "stained glass" effect.
4. Hang your "Stained Glass" Heart in a sunny window.

Alternate activity: Cut the heart out and color the white sections with crayon or markers.

CHAPTER 12

Traumatic Events and Illnesses

 ## Challenge

The child has experienced a traumatic event or illness.

Goals

The child will regain a sense of safety.

The child will process feelings and memories related to the trauma or illness.

The child will have at least one way to stay connected to loved ones while the child recovers from the trauma or illness.

Skill: Coping with traumatic events and illnesses

Skills included in this chapter comprise talking about the traumatic event or illness, identifying feelings attached to the experience, recognizing fears and worries, identifying motivators for getting through the healing process, creating personal goals, maintaining connections to loved ones when hospitalized, and recognizing any positives from the experience.

✚ Interventions

CARDBOARD HOUSES AND BUILDINGS

Cardboard Houses and Buildings is an activity for counselors working with children affected by trauma and traumatic illness. The child creates cardboard buildings that are replicas of buildings connected to the traumatic event or illness. The activity serves a few different clinical purposes: the completed buildings can be used to provide a visual way for the child to recall and communicate some details of the event or illness; the child and counselor can have a dialogue about the event while the activity is being done; and the completed buildings can be used in sand tray work, play therapy activities, and used as part of a trauma narrative.

Buildings may include: homes that the child lived in or visited (e.g. an apartment, a homeless shelter, a foster home, a group home, a tent, a camper, etc.), a school, a hospital, the police station, a fire station, a youth corrections facility, a doctor's office, buildings belonging to a crime scene, prison (e.g. if a child has visited a parent in prison), a rehabilitation center, etc.

Materials

- Various sized recycled boxes
- Scissors
- Paper
- Crayons and markers
- Glue

Directions

- Brainstorm with the child: What buildings come to mind when you remember the traumatic event (refer to the specific event)?
- Choose one building to start with and choose a box for that building.
- Cut out pieces of paper to match the front and sides of each box.
- Have the child decorate the front and sides of the building.
- Glue the completed picture of the front of the building to the front of the box. Glue any completed sides of the building to the sides of the box.
- Decide if and/or how you will label the building.

- Discuss what memories or details arise in thinking about, and re-creating, this building.

- Make as many buildings as necessary that are helpful for the child.

ENVELOPE HOUSES AND BUILDINGS

Envelope Houses and Buildings are similar to the previous activity, except the child draws the buildings onto paper envelopes instead of cardboard boxes. The advantage of using envelopes is they are easier to store and/or transport, and they can hold actual stories and narratives. The disadvantage is they are not as easy to use in sand tray activities (the envelopes get sand stuck in them) and they are harder to use in some play therapy activities because they are flat and less interactive.

Materials

- Various envelopes of size, color, and texture

- Crayons and markers

- Paper

Directions

- Brainstorm with the child: What buildings come to mind when you remember that event (refer to the specific traumatic event)?

- Choose one building to start with and choose an envelope for that building.

- Decorate the envelope to look like the building.

- Discuss: What details and memories come up for you when you think about this building? What feelings arise?

- You and the child can write and illustrate any details on paper, then fold the paper up to go into the envelope.

BAND AID AND BOO BOO STORIES

Many traumatic experiences involve physical and/or emotional pain. Band Aid and Boo Boo Stories are a way for younger kids to tell the story about their traumatic experiences.

Materials

- Band aids of various sizes

- Markers and crayons

- Paper

Directions

Before starting the activity explain how people can feel "hurt" in many ways— our bodies can feel hurt when we get injuries, illnesses, or other "boo boos," but our hearts and our feelings can also feel hurt when we experience something sad, scary, or infuriating.

Have the child draw a picture from the traumatic event. Give them as much time as they need to create the picture.

Ask the child if there is anything they want to share with you about the picture. You can also ask if it's okay for you to ask questions about it.

Before going to the next step, if it's at all possible, ask the child if they would like a photocopy of their picture. (The next part of the activity involves adding band aids to the picture and sometimes children don't want to alter their original artwork unless they have a copy first.)

Provide a variety of band aid styles and designs. Prompt the child to put band aids anywhere on the picture where someone or something needs healing. For example, the child might put a band aid on someone's body where they got hurt; they might put one on a building or a vehicle that got damaged; or they might put them over the hearts of people who got scared or saddened by what they saw.

If you like, take the activity one step further and say: "Now that you have shown all of the areas that need some healing, let's imagine sending love to all of those parts and places to help them heal."

TONGUE DEPRESSOR WORRY DOLLS

Worry Dolls, as noted earlier, are a comforting activity for a child because they create a doll that can "listen" to their worries, "hold onto" their worries, or simply be a comforting object to hold when they are worried.

Tongue depressors are my least favorite medium for making worry dolls, but when you have a child who ends up in hospital under urgent circumstances, you have to use what you have available (unless by some miracle you just so happened to grab a crafting kit on your way to the hospital in an emergency). That being said, be creative with the supplies you do find on hand, and ask the hospital staff if there are additional supplies available. Here are some suggestions for materials you can find in hospital:

- *Tongue depressor:* Use as the main body of the worry doll.

- *Band aids and adhesive bandages:* Use these like you would use tape.

- *Cotton swabs/Q-tips:* Remove the cotton to use as hair for the doll; use the stick for arms.

- *Paper towels from the dispenser:* Use for making clothing. If there are no scissors around, tear the towels for rudimentary fabric and/or to wrap around the doll.

- *Pens:* Use a pen to draw a face onto the doll. Decorate a paper towel with a design before tearing it into pieces for "clothing." Write the child's worry onto the tongue depressor before making the doll.

- *String:* Knitting has become so popular, especially in hospital waiting rooms, that you just might get lucky and find someone willing to share a piece for a child's worry doll. If you do find some string, it can be used for the doll's hair, but also to tie the doll's clothing onto the doll. If you carry dental floss in your purse, you can use that as well.

- *Paper:* Paper from a magazine, from your purse or bag, or from a registration slip can be made into dolls' clothing and accessories. You only need small strips of paper because the dolls are so narrow and small. Strips of paper can be curled or folded accordion style to make curly hair; it can be folded tightly to make arm shapes; and if the paper is sturdy enough, a thin strip can be used to "tie" clothing or arms into place until you find something better to do so.

- *Straws:* If you have scissors, you can trim straws for arms, or cut small segments of straws to make beads for a necklace for the doll.

- *Crayons:* Check the waiting room for a children's area that may have coloring books and crayons. Borrow a couple of crayons for making the doll and then return them.

Be as resourceful and creative as you can with the supplies you have on hand. The child will most likely appreciate the normalcy of making a craft or knowing that you are doing it. The worry doll might be a comfort in the moment as well.

MY WISH TREE

Use the accompanying worksheets to complete a Wish Tree. The child colors the Wish Tree and then decorates each leaf to say or show something they wish for in the near future. Here are some leaf examples:

- Get out of the hospital soon.

- Feel safe again.

- Go to my favorite restaurant again.

- See my family and friends.

My
wish
tree

*

Leaves for your wish tree –

1. Write wishes on the leaves

2. Color the leaves in with lighter colors

3. Color your wish tree (use a darker color for the tree crown if you like contrast between your tree and leaves)

4. glue the leaves onto the tree

Wish Tree Leaves

- Celebrate.

- Be healthy.

- Laugh again.

- Play that new video game.

- Go back to school.

Of course, sometimes children will focus on material things, but it is up to you how you structure the activity, if at all. A counselor or social worker may approach this activity differently than a parent or care provider, so keep in mind that the activity is flexible. The main goal of this activity is to create a visual piece of art that the child can hang up somewhere so they can be reminded of the things they are looking forward to if and when this time in their life starts to improve.

I have also done this activity with children where the goal is to express wishes for others, rather than themselves. In the event of a tragedy in which several people are affected, a child can feel helpless and even hopeless. A Wish Tree is an opportunity for the child to express what they would give to those affected if they could. For example, the entire tree could represent a wish for peace and healing. Each leaf on the tree could have a person's name on it (typically, the victims of the event or those affected by the event).

ACCORDION-STYLE VISION BOARDS

Vision Boards are a visual display depicting any variety of themes including: "What motivates you?", "Where would you love to travel?", "What are you grateful for?", "How do you want your life to look five years from now?", "What are your goals in life?", "Things that make me smile".

Most of the time, Vision Boards are done on a flat surface such as a poster board, but in this activity we make them accordion style. The advantage of Accordion-style Vision Boards is they are more compact and easier to transport if the child is homeless, in a hospital, or in some other confined or transitory environment.

Materials

- Paper

- Scissors

- Recycled cardboard (e.g. from a cracker box)

- Glue

- Markers and/or crayons

- Images, words, or phrases cut from magazines (optional)

Directions

- Cut paper into strips of equal width—they can be whatever size you need them to be, but on average about 4 in (10 cm) in height is best. Tape the strips of paper together to create an extended length of paper.

- Fold the strip of paper accordion style until you reach the length and number of pages you want inside the board. (Accordion style means you fold the paper over to make a page, then fold it back in the opposite direction to the same size as the page before, and then continue folding back and forth in this manner.)

- Cut two pieces of cardboard the same size as the book pages.

- Glue one piece of cardboard to the outermost flap of paper and the other piece of cardboard to the outermost flap of paper. This will create a "cover" for the book.

- Decorate the cover and pages with any pictures and words that inspire and motivate the child. The pictures and words can relate to positive feelings, happy memories, goals, wishes, hopes, dreams, places the child wants to travel to someday, activities they love doing, etc.

Accordion-style Vision Boards can be used to remind the child of various things, such as the following:

- Everyday moments in life that they are thankful for and/or that bring them joy. This can be helpful for children facing chronic illnesses or constant change.

- What they have to live for or look forward to. This works especially well with children faced with depression, acute medical challenges, and/or going through major changes and upheaval.

- What their long-term goals are. This works well with children who have challenges with their attention span, and/or have experienced a traumatic event (emotional or physical) that has affected their ability to recall or retain information.

- What is good in the world. Some children experience deprivation, violence, neglect, war, etc. on a daily basis. They have had limited exposure to what is actually good in this world. For these children, accordion books that show stories and images of people showing kindness is especially helpful.

MATCHBOX PHOENIX

A phoenix is a legendary bird that allows itself to perish in flames and is then reborn from the fire. The phoenix, therefore, regenerates its life by embracing the fire and coming out alive and renewed. For this reason, the phoenix has become a metaphor for embracing life's challenges and coming out the other side better and stronger.

It can be daunting for anyone to look at a major life challenge as being an impetus for growth and "rebirth," but it can be especially so for children. A Matchbox Phoenix is a creative activity that reminds the child of the possibility of that renewed identity.

Prior to doing this activity, gather some stories about people who have found strength and hope from a similar challenge to the one the child is experiencing. Do an online search, for example, to find celebrities and others who have experienced what the child is going through. When children hear that others have suffered terrible loss or experiences and have not only survived, but have become happier and healthier people because of it, this can be a source of inspiration and help them to persevere and see a glimmer of hope.

If you are working with younger children, a butterfly or snake may be a better metaphor to use, as it is not as dramatic and graphic. You can make a Matchbox Butterfly or Matchbox Snake with younger children and use the example of how the butterfly and snake have so much more freedom and joy in their lives once they move past the major transition in their life (transitioning from caterpillar to butterfly; a snake shedding its skin).

The child can put the Matchbox Phoenix in a school locker, on a windowsill at home, or in a backpack, etc. as a reminder that even if things feel impossible and dark at the moment, there is the possibility to thrive later on.

Materials

- Matchbox Phoenix activity page

- Markers and crayons

- Scissors

- Glue

- Small box-style matchbox (the kind that has a drawer that slides in and out of the box)

Directions

- Color the phoenix, butterfly, or snake.

- Cut them out where indicated and glue them to the inside drawer of the matchbox.

- Color the strip of paper that will wrap around the outside of the box. Cut it out and glue it to the outside frame of the matchbox.

Matchbox Phoenix

Directions:

1. Choose a strip below for making a "Matchbox Phoenix"— you can make a phoenix, butterfly, or snake.
2. Color the strip you chose and then cut it out.
3. Fold the strip along the 2 dotted lines where noted.
4. Glue the bottom section of the strip to the bottom of the matchbox tray as noted.
5. Next, color the cover strip and cut it out.
6. Fold the cover strip where noted and glue it to the outside of your matchbox.
7. Allow the glue to dry.

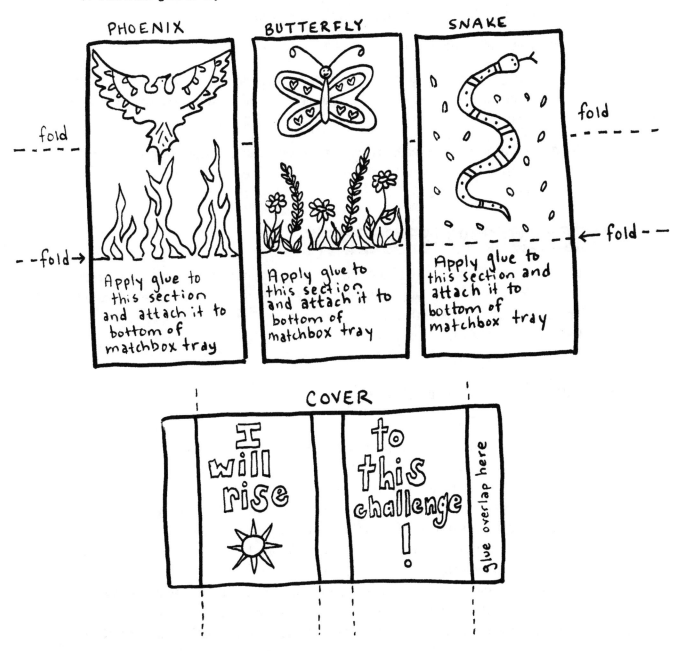

DECORATING CASTS, WRAPS, AND BANDAGES

Ask the child's medical care provider what options there are, if any, for the child to decorate any medical bandages and casts. Many of us are used to the standard tradition of having friends and family draw on casts, but there are more options when/if the medical provider gives the okay. Here are options to consider and ask about, if appropriate:

- Use temporary tattoos to decorate casts.

- Sew or embroider designs into dressings.

- Get a custom cast design (e.g. with superhero badges).

- Get a 3D printed cast.

- Design and create your own artwork for the cast or bandage—run a search online for "cool cast art" or "cast designs" if you need some inspiration and ideas.

- Use band aids to create art that can go on other bandages (e.g. three criss-crossing band aids will make a butterfly shape that can be colored with permanent markers).

LETTERS AND CARDS FROM HOME

Decorate a shoebox or other container for a hospitalized child to store any cards and letters from friends, family, and classmates. When the child is feeling rested or well enough to look at their mail, it will be easy to find. The box can also be a keepsake for all of those correspondences.

 # An accompanying story
The Dark Cloud

Carlos was riding his bike to the park one day when suddenly a dark cloud appeared. The cloud was large and swirling with angry colors. The cloud made sharp, loud noises that shook the ground. The cloud released bolts of lightning that made flashes of light across the sky. And all of this made Carlos feel so very frightened. Carlos got off of his bike and found shelter until the storm stopped.

When the dark cloud disappeared, Carlos finished riding his bike to the park. His friends were waiting for him to play.

But Carlos did not want to play any longer. Carlos was still frightened by the dark cloud and the storm and he was scared it was going to come back.

Carlos asked one of his friends if he had also seen the dark cloud. His friend said yes he had, and he described the same cloud and storm that Carlos had seen.

They talked about how frightening the cloud and the storm had been. They talked about the scary loud noises, the flashes of lights, and the feeling of fear they felt as it was all happening.

As they were sharing their stories about the storm, Carlos noticed that talking to his friend helped him feel much better. It felt good to know someone else had experienced the same thing and even had some of the same feelings.

Carlos's friend then gave Carlos some good advice. He said he had experienced the dark cloud even before today. He said if the dark cloud ever came again, there were things Carlos could do to feel a little better! First and foremost he could make sure he was safe (finding shelter was a good idea!), and once he was safe, he would help others who needed help. This is a great way to feel less scared of the dark cloud, his friend said. He also said that once the dark cloud passes, it is helpful to talk to others about what happened.

Carlos took a few moments to take deep breaths and look around. He could see that the sun was coming out. He could hear birds starting to sing again. He could hear a basketball bouncing against the blacktop. He could hear and see signs that the storm had passed. Carlos knew it was time to get back to enjoying what he could of the day.

 ## An activity to go along with the story

MY UMBRELLA WORKSHEET

My Umbrella is a worksheet that children can use to identify a "dark cloud" (something that happened to the child that they didn't like and/or that frightened them), as well as identify their "umbrella" (people, places, and things that help them feel safer or less frightened).

 ## Affirmations

✓ This will pass.

✓ This moment is temporary.

✓ I am surrounded by love and people who care about me.

✓ I am getting better.

✓ I am going to get through this.

✓ I make the best of each day.

"My Umbrella" Worksheet

Name your "dark cloud." Your dark cloud is something that happens to you that you do not like, or that frightens you.

Use the sections of the umbrella to write down things that help you feel safer when your "dark cloud" happens.

CHAPTER 13

Family Challenges

. . . .

Tight Budgets and Poverty

! ## Challenge

The child's family is struggling financially.

◎ ## Goal

The child and family will utilize what they do have for resources to make the best of their situation.

⚙ ## Skills: Coping with tight budgets and poverty

Skills addressed include valuing time together; providing "no cost" rewards and incentives for children, making toys and projects together, and budgeting as a family.

✚ Interventions

TIME, NOT THINGS

One cannot underestimate the impact of living with limited to no income—many of the problems that arise as a result seem insurmountable. I cannot emphasize enough how corrosive this level of stress can be to a family.

However, one valuable resource that is available to families, regardless of income, is time. The beautiful thing about time is that it's something we all have to give. And in all of the years I have worked with families and children, the one thing kids have consistently wanted more of is their parents' time. They want their parents' love and attention. They want to be noticed and praised for the things they are doing well. They want their parents to turn off the TV and any devices, and spend some quality time with them. And this doesn't cost a thing.

I know from experience that trying to relay this message to parents can be met with resistance or disbelief (e.g. "my child wants more video games" or "my child wants those expensive shoes"). And yes, that is probably true. However, oftentimes parents and kids need the reminder that *time* is a valued commodity as well. The parent may not be able to provide expensive shoes, but the parent can provide half an hour of doing something together like drawing pictures or building a pillow fort. If you are a professional working with families, support the notion that parents and guardians still have the most valuable gift of all—time spent with the child.

"NO COST" INCENTIVES FOR CHILDREN

If you are a counselor or other professional who works with children, then you are familiar with the effectiveness of making incentive plans for children. Sticker charts are a great example of an incentive plan—the child earns stickers for positive behaviors such as using the toilet (during potty training) or completing chores. Incentive plans work well for encouraging a child to carry out the behaviors you want.

One challenge, however, is that many incentive plans are based on "things" the child earns in return for the positive behaviors (e.g. stickers, treats, a trip to the ice cream shop, or even a video game). I created a handout of "No Cost" Incentives for Children for the families that want to (or have to) use incentives that do not involve monetary rewards. In addition to using this handout for incentives, it's also a great resource for ways to spend time with children without spending any money.

"No Cost" Incentives for Children

- I can stay up 15 minutes past my bedtime tonight.

- I can choose a board game to play with my parent/guardian.

- I get to pick out a movie to watch with my parent/guardian.

- I get to talk to my parent/guardian for 10 minutes without being interrupted or asked any questions.

- My parent/guardian will color with me for 15 minutes.

- I get to take a walk with my parent/guardian.

- My parent/guardian and I get to bake something yummy together.

- I get to choose where I sit at the table tonight.

- I get 15 additional minutes of screen time on this day: _____.

- My parent/guardian will watch me build or create something for 15 minutes.

- My parent/guardian will read aloud to me for 15 minutes at bedtime on this night: _____.

- I get to choose a dessert for tomorrow night.

- I don't have to do my chore for tomorrow.

- I get to have a bubble bath tonight.

- My parent/guardian will have a tea party with me (with snacks and drinks already in the house).

- My parent/guardian will go on a night walk with me.

*

- My parent/guardian will look at the night sky/look for constellations with me.

- My parent/guardian will help me build a fort out of blankets and pillows.

- My parent/guardian will have a snack with me in my fort, in the tree house, or outdoors.

- My parent/guardian will do my hair in a special way tomorrow morning.

- Other ideas:

_____

_____

_____

_____

_____

_____

_____

_____

_____

_____

_____

_____

_____

_____

_____

MAKE YOUR OWN TOYS

When you live on a budget or have limited income, it's a challenge to hear your children asking for things you can't afford. Shelter, food, and clothing take precedence over the need for toys.

That being said, as I mentioned before, time is a valued commodity and you can use your time to make fun toys with your kids or clients. Not only do they end up with something they can play with, but more importantly you build memories of that time spent together.

There are endless project ideas on the internet and in books about ways to use recycled materials to create simple toys and even decorate playful spaces. Dollhouses, superhero figurines, blocks, games, toy vehicles, roads, etc. can all be made from recycled goods. You can also decorate a child's sleeping or play area with fun artwork and designs made from recycled items.

Use the internet or your local library to find specific project ideas. Here are some helpful keywords to research: DIY toys (DIY means "do it yourself"); toys from recycled materials; cardboard tube crafts; cereal box crafts; cracker box crafts; toys from trash.

In the meantime, encourage the families you work with to save recycled materials for creative projects. It may also help to remind them that, even though kids often want the same toys that their friends have, they can also get satisfaction from having toys that no one else has.

BUDGET AS A FAMILY

Budgeting is typically planned and executed by the adults in the home, but children can learn and apply the basic concepts of budgeting too.

Here are some step-by-step suggestions about budgeting as a family:

1. The adults have an initial conversation to discuss how much money comes into the household each month, and how much goes out. This can be a tough conversation to have, so plan ahead for added support or incentives to get through this initial stage. Use online resources to find free templates or apps that help you outline your income and expenses.

2. The adults should have a good idea of where their income is going. The next step is to review those expenses to find where spending can be cut back. Again, this is a tough conversation and the adults involved should plan ahead for ways to manage the dialogue and plan what to do if things get emotional or stressful.

3. Once the adults have an idea of what the budget looks like, it is good practice to include the kids in a family meeting about the basics of budgeting. For example, define what a budget is and why it is important: "A budget is a way that we figure out how much money we have to spend on the things we need, like food, rent, and clothing. It is also used to help us figure out how much money we have, if any, to spend on things we want. The budget is based on the amount of money we get from our jobs and/or benefits. It's important to have a budget to make sure we don't spend more money than we have, otherwise we won't be able to pay for the things we need."

4. Inform the children about what they need to know about the current budget. For example: "We will not have any extra money for a while because we need to pay some bills that will take some time to pay off. This means, for now, we will have to be creative about how we spend our money on things we *need*, like food. It also means we won't be able to spend money on the things we *want* right now, like going to the movies. Instead, we can have a game night and pop popcorn, or come up with other ways to spend time together that don't cost money." In another example, the family might have a limited amount of money to spend on "extras" each month, but needs to decide as a family how to split that up or decide where it goes.

When you are trying to budget:

*   Let your children know that topics related to how much money your family makes or spends is usually a private matter. If the children are young or not able to respect boundaries around private information yet, then do not share specific information about your finances.

*   Use online resources for ways to budget and save money.

*   Consider using case management services or community supports to help the family create and follow a budget.

*   Ask community members or look online for what is available in your community for free or reduced cost clothing, medical care, or food.

Building Relationships

 ## Challenge

Family members are struggling to connect with one another, either due to discord or physical distance.

 ## Goals

The child will feel more connected to the family (or a specific family member).

Many families find themselves struggling to connect with one another due to multiple challenges. Consider these examples:

- A single parent works all day and then goes to college classes at night and doesn't have the time she desires to spend with her children.

- A parent is working multiple jobs.

- A parent is in the military and is away from home for long periods of time.

- A parent has a chronic illness and is fatigued, ill, or at the hospital much of the time.

- The parents are divorced and have children who have busy schedules—both parents wish they had more time to connect with their kids.

In these situations it can be challenging to establish and maintain family cohesion. But here are some strategies for building those relationships even when there are obstacles.

 ## Skill: Building relationships

Skills addressed include creating opportunities for connection, staying connected, communicating with family, sharing and showing love, and creating a schedule for daily to weekly connection.

 ## Interventions

SHARED JOURNALS

A Shared Journal is exactly what it sounds like—it's a journal shared between two family members. The journal is used to communicate positive messages and update each other. It's also a place to ask questions, check in, and make plans for events and activities you look forward to. The journal is *not* a place to leave notes about chores that need to get done, or to inform the other about disciplinary issues (e.g. "You're grounded for the next week" or "Oh, by the way I got a detention in math class today"). The journal is meant to build and maintain a positive connection with each other. The communication that happens within the journal is meant to support relationship building.

Purchase or make a blank journal. Agree to keep the journal in the same spot all the time so that either of you can find it whenever it's needed or wanted. If it's helpful, establish at least one time a week when each person will check the journal (e.g. Jane will check the journal on Sunday mornings, Mom will check it on Sunday nights). However, the journal can be accessed and used at any time of the week.

Here are some ways to use the Shared Journal (also see the Shared Journal Prompts sheet):

- Ask questions about each other to get to know each other better. Use the handout provided to get ideas for the kinds of questions you might want to ask.

- Write down the positive things you notice your child doing. Let them know you are proud of them. For example: "You studied so hard for your test— I'm so proud of you!"

- Let your child know you appreciate the little and big things they do. For example: "I really appreciate you being patient in the grocery store last night!"

- Put in a quote, poem, or song lyrics you think your child might like, or that might help them through a tough day.

- Draw silly pictures for your child.

- Put something unexpected in there, such as a sticker or fun tattoo.

As you can see, all of the above foster a sense of fun and positive connection.

Shared Journal Prompts

- What is a song that describes the week you are having so far?

- Where is your favorite place to go out to eat? What do you like about the decorations or the "feel" of that place? What are your favorite things to eat there?

- Draw a stick figure of yourself doing something funny.

- Tell me what you like about me.

- What's the greatest challenge you have overcome so far in your life? How did you get through that?

- What helps you feel safe and calm?

- What are your favorite snacks for a movie?

- When was the last time you cried? What made you cry?

- What is something I do that makes you feel proud of me?

- Pretend we had a day for just you and me and we had only $10 to spend for the day. How would you want to spend the day together?

- If you were an animal, what animal would you be?

- If you could pack anything for a picnic, what would you pack? Where would you want to have a picnic?

- Name three places you would love to travel to. What would you want to do in these three places?

- Draw or list your favorite candies.

- Name a color that describes your personality? How so?

*

- What is a favorite Halloween costume you've worn?

- Name someone who makes you feel uncomfortable. What does that person do that makes you feel uncomfortable?

- If you were a flower, what kind of flower would you be?

- Describe a recurring dream you've had (in the past or current).

- Draw your family as animals—they can be any kind of animals.

- What is your "dream car"?

- Who has inspired you recently?

- Draw an octopus eating a cupcake.

- When was the last time someone yelled at you or said something unkind to you? Describe what happened. Did that person apologize?

- Describe a house that you like (in real life).

- List three things you are grateful for today.

- Draw a monster.

- Name a book, song, or piece of art that describes you and/or your life.

- Name a movie you like. Why do you like it?

- What do you think are appropriate and fair rules for a *responsible* pre-teen (age 10–12)?

- What do you think are appropriate and fair rules for a pre-teen who is still learning to be responsible?

- If you could change one thing about your personality what would you change?

- How do you like to celebrate your birthday?

- Draw a picture of me (the child draws the adult, the adult draws the child).

- Are you more like a sunrise or a sunset? How so?

- Describe your favorite breakfast.

- What are your favorite family meals or desserts?

- When you are sick, how do you prefer to be taken care of? What can others do to help you feel better?

- When you are crying, what helps you to feel better?

- Who are you most alike in the family? How so?

- Draw your family as flowers in a garden.

- Describe your favorite ice cream dessert.

- Draw a picture of us.

- Write a poem about us.

- What is your favorite thing about each season—winter, spring, summer, and fall?

- Tell me about a happy moment you've had recently.

- Tell me what your day is usually like.

- Three things I appreciate about you today are…

- If you could give me anything in the world, what would you give to me?

- What are your favorite things to do and to eat at a fair or amusement park?

- Add your own journal prompts here:

_____

_____

_____

_____

_____

_____

_____

CREATING CONNECTIONS TOGETHER, APART

When family members cannot be together physically, there are still ways they can connect and even do projects together, but apart. If one family member is hospitalized, incarcerated, deployed, or away for another reason, then consider one of the following activities to maintain some connection between family members.

If you have internet access:

- Use email, Skype, and other venues to communicate with each other.

- Write a story, song, poem, or memoir together. Create a word document that can be shared back and forth. Decide how each will contribute to the writing (e.g. one person writes a section and then sends it to the other family member to create the next section).

- Create shared boards on Pinterest—the boards can be based on shared humor, a desire to travel or explore a certain place together, crafts you want to create together, a passion for the same hobby or interest (e.g. race cars), or things you want to do together when you are reunited (e.g. movies you want to see, a restaurant to try, a day trip).

- Play a video game together online, or play the same game separately but use it as a shared experience to talk about (e.g. what levels have been the most challenging).

If you do not have internet access:

- Read the same book (or books) while you are apart. When you are reunited, you can discuss what you liked and didn't like about the book, something you learned from the book, and points of interest about the characters, events, or places in the book.

- Keep a journal for each other—whenever you miss the other person or want to tell them something, do so by writing about it in the journal. Some days might be messages like "I missed you today," whereas other days you might want to share something that happened or something that reminded you of the other person. Next time you are reunited you can give that person the journal.

- Send written letters. If you are at all creative, try your hand at mail art to make the exchange of letters even more interesting. Mail art simply means you create artwork on the outside of your envelopes.

TIME IN

A Time In is an alternative to a "time out." As soon as you notice your child is starting to test limits or become grumpy or reactive, try a Time In. A Time In is when you honor the need for you and the child to connect. It means communicating to the child: "I notice a disconnect here—something is not working for us at the moment. Let's have a Time In." A Time In can mean anything from having hot cocoa together, giving the child a foot massage, coloring a page in a coloring book together, or snuggling on the couch while you watch a cartoon on TV. A Time In is a chance to disengage from a pattern of communication that isn't working and to engage in an activity that builds your connection instead.

TO THE CASTLE GAME

This game has questions for players about thoughts and feelings. It also provides opportunities for players to talk about life experiences. Playing games with children is a wonderful way to connect with them and build relationships.

Note: Use the playing pieces on page 82 if needed.

LOVE NOTES

Love Notes are written messages that a parent or guardian leaves for the child in various places, such as in the child's lunchbox, in their school backpack, on the bathroom mirror, or next to their laptops and smartphones. Love Notes are a great way to remind children how loved and special they are, and a way to build your connection to each other.

My favorite Love Notes are the ones that go in children's packed snacks or lunches. Use the handout for ideas to make Love Notes positive and fun.

FAMILY DINNERS

Plan at least one family dinner a week where the family sits down to share a meal (indoor picnics work as well!). It sounds simplistic, yet Family Dinners seem to be happening less and less. Children often enjoy Family Dinners as part of their weekly routine and as a way to connect with their loved ones.

If your family has a hard time figuring out what to talk about once sitting down to a meal, use the handout for Dinner Conversation Cards. You can cut out the Conversation Cards, add them to a bowl or a jar, and then place them on the dinner table. Have one of the kids pick a Conversation Card and go from there.

END

START

TO THE CASTLE game

TO THE CASTLE

Materials needed:

· A coin
· Your own game pieces (i.e. bottle caps or game pieces from another game). You can also photocopy and color your own from the Game Pieces page in this book.

Directions:

· Youngest player goes first
· The player flips the coin. "Heads" = move 1 space. "Tails" = move 2 spaces.
· When you move your piece, you will land on a picture. Follow the chart below to answer the questions that go with each picture.
· The first player to make it to the castle wins the game.

 Make a comment about someone who loves you or cares about you.

 Talk about something or someone that makes you feel happy.

 If you could give a wish to anyone but yourself, what would you wish for and who would you give it to?

 Describe a moment or memory that you wish you could experience again.

Talk about a time when you had to make a tough (or important) decision.

 Tell about a time you got angry.

 Talk about a time when you felt like you didn't belong.

 What is something that scares you?

 Describe a time when you got really sick or hurt.

 Describe a moment when you felt proud of something you did.

 Talk about a time that someone made a promise to you. Did that person keep their promise?

Love Notes

For non-readers

- Put a sticker on a small piece of paper.

- Draw a heart and sign it.

- Draw a picture for your child—it can be a simple picture of a ladybug, a rainbow, stick figures, a sun for a sunny day, a flower, an animal face, a smiley face, a heart, etc.

- Cut out a picture from a magazine or catalogue and glue it to a note (e.g. cut out a picture of the child's favorite animal from a magazine).

- Thumbprint pictures—color your thumb with marker and then make a thumbprint on the note paper. Turn your thumbprint into a drawing, such as a person, a kitten, a pig, a flower, a bumble bee, or an octopus.

- On holidays and special days, draw something related to the day.

- If your child is in preschool or kindergarten and is learning via "units" or curriculum themes, add a picture related to what they are learning about. For example, if your child is learning about seasons, draw something related to the season. If your child is learning about numbers, write the number and draw the corresponding number of ducks, polka dots, hearts, etc. to go with it.

For beginner readers

- I love you!

- Have a good day!

- Good luck!

- Smile!

- See you later!

- You are loved!

- Have a happy day!

- Have fun today!

*

- Yay! It's Friday!
- Yay! It's gym day!
- Yay! It's art day!
- Yay! It's book day/library day!
- Yay! It's a trip day!

- Yay! It's music day!
- You can do it!
- You are my sunshine!
- You are a cool kid!

Interactive note ideas for beginner readers

If your child is responsible as well as an efficient eater, then it can be fun to include a small pencil and one of the following interactive notes in their lunchbox. These ideas work best for those kids who are given plenty of time to eat their lunches at their schools or daycare.

- Draw a shape, a doodle, or a scribble mark and have your child finish it.
- Pack a super simple connect-the-dot.

Notes for older readers

There may be a point at which your child feels embarrassed or too old to be getting notes in their lunches. Be mindful of this and support their boundaries. The notes in this section are geared toward kids who might be reaching that phase—these notes are meant to be less personal (fewer "I love you" notes) and more interactive or able to be shared with friends.

If your child is excited about a subject, put facts about that subject on their lunch note. These could be facts about a topic (e.g. sharks, skateboarding, hula hoops), facts about their favorite video game (e.g. who designed it, changes that were made to the original design, or how old the designer was when they designed it), facts about world records, or any other fact you think your child might find interesting.

Jokes: You can find jokes online and print them or write them out for a note. The great thing about finding jokes online is that some sites will even allow you to search the jokes by topic. This is especially helpful if your child loves a certain subject or if you want a joke for a special occasion (e.g. birthday, first day of school).

Secret codes: You can find child-friendly secret codes online (type the keywords "secret code," "secret codes for kids" into your browser) or design your own. Include the key to the code with your note—your child can decipher the note using this.

Puzzle: Turn your note into a five-piece puzzle that the child can put together at lunchtime.

Riddles: Write a riddle on the lunch note. If your child hasn't figured it out by the time they get home, give them the answer.

Clues: Treat the lunch notes as a series of clues to something your child has to guess. For example, Monday's note might say: "It has four legs." If the child hasn't guessed what you are thinking of, then leave a note in Tuesday's lunch, such as "It likes to eat leaves," and carry on this way until the child guesses it.

Optical illusion: Add one of these to your child's lunch note. Children love optical illusions and they are fun to share with friends. You can find them online (search "optical illusions") or photocopy one from a book.

Interactive notes: Your child might already share their notes with friends at the table, but these notes in particular encourage them to do so. You will need to include a small pencil with these notes (make sure the child is responsible enough, and allowed, to bring a pencil in their lunchbox). Here are some interactive notes:

- Find someone next to you who will draw a cat on this piece of paper. Have them autograph their picture.

- Find out who has the messiest, neatest, most creative, etc. handwriting at your table. Have each person who is willing to play, write the word "Superhero" on the paper and then choose someone else at the table to judge the winners.

- Take a poll: Draw columns on your child's note and then include questions. For example: "What do you like more, cake or cookies?" or "Who is a better singer, _____ or _____?" (Ask questions within your child's area of interest or sense of humor.)

- Draw a tic-tac-toe board on the note and tell your child to challenge someone to a game at lunchtime.

- Have a "note for everyone" day where you include additional notes for your child's friends that they sit with.

*

Dinner Conversation Cards

What is the favorite pair of shoes you've ever had?

Tell me about something funny or strange that happened this week.

What song best describes your day today?

What is your favorite dessert?

What time of the day does your mind and body feel the calmest?
Why is this?

What is something a friend does that makes you laugh?

When was the last time you had a clumsy moment? Did you get embarrassed?

Do you like to sing?

*

When do you feel shy?

What is something you did really well today?

Who do you like to spend time with? Why?

If you could travel to any place right now, where would you go? Why?

What are some of your favorite smells?

If you had the time and money to learn something new, what would it be?

Who do you wish you could spend more time with? Why?

Name a place where you feel relaxed and/or safe.

Name three colors that describe your mood today.

*

What is your favorite flavor of ice cream?

What kind of candy best matches your personality?

What is something your friends are talking about lately?

Who is the kindest person you know?

Who is the funniest person you know?

WEEKLY FAMILY MEETINGS

Weekly Family Meetings may sound "old school" but they are a highly effective means for families to address issues such as rules, upcoming important dates, family news, changes, etc. They also provide a regular and predictable time when children can count on their family being together. We often underestimate the importance of gathering an entire family in one space simply to talk, recognize/recap, and plan ahead.

Here is a simple outline for a family meeting.

1. *Talk:* Each person checks in about how their week was. High and low points of the week can be noted; accomplishments can be announced; and adding agenda items can also be addressed.

2. *Recognize/recap:* One of the adults recaps any accomplishments. For example: "Before we move on, I just want to say again how proud I am that Sarah got a B on her paper and that Scout was kind to someone on the bus today."

3. *Plan ahead:* Family members share any events coming up in the following week such as appointments, celebrations, community events, or family outings.

4. *Miscellaneous:* Last, go over any agenda items that have been added to the list. For example, Scout might want to advocate for a later bedtime on Saturdays.

Helpful tips for family meetings:

- Spend the first family meeting coming up with, and agreeing on, basic rules for the meetings. For example: such as one person speaks at a time, the meeting lasts no longer than one hour, be respectful, etc.

- If family members have a hard time following a "one person speaks at a time" rule, consider using a talking stick or other object that is held by the person whose turn it is to speak. The object could be a ball of yarn, a figurine, or a salt shaker—almost any object can be made into the family meeting mascot for a talking stick.

- Have a special snack planned for during or after the meeting and/or provide chewing gum to help fidgety members settle into the meeting.

PARENT REPORT CARDS

Parent Report Cards give children a chance to communicate their thoughts and feelings about how they feel their parents are doing with key parental responsibilities.

As there are many ways to define a parent's job, I have left the template blank. I have added a list of various responsibilities, but the parent and/or child ultimately decide what will go on the Parent Report Card.

Parent Report Cards work best with families in which there is already communication between the child and parent and/or a willingness on the parent's part to engage in this activity. That being said, it is also an activity that supports the parenting role because the child and parent have a discussion about what parenting is. And by parenting, I mean the basics—not, for example, "My parent/guardian buys me all the toys and video games I want."

Try the following Parent Report Card suggestions:

My parent/guardian…

- makes sure there is a roof over my head.

- makes sure I have a meal to eat at least _____ times a day.

- makes sure I get at least _____ hours of sleep each night (which is the recommended hours of sleep needed for kids my age).

- makes sure I have clean clothes to wear.

- keeps me safe.

- helps me learn and use good manners/be respectful to others.

- reminds me I am a great kid.

- tells me they love me at least once a day.

- reminds me of what I am good at; gives me praise for the good things I do.

- reads to me each day.

- encourages me to do my best.

- asks me questions about my day, such as who I had lunch with or how my test went in class.

- has met my closest friends and their parents.

- checks in with my teacher at least once a month to make sure I am doing what I'm supposed to in school.

- asks me what I am interested in.

PARENT REPORT CARD

Parent name: _____ Date: _____

Parent role /responsibility	Grade	How can parent improve? Comments

A: Excellent job!

B: My parent is doing a good job with this.

C: My parent is doing okay/average with this.

D: My parent is not doing their job with this, and/or needs a lot of improvement.

- provides basic house rules and/or routine so that I know what's expected of me at home.

- brings me to the doctor when I am sick or need medical care.

- makes sure I take good care of my body (teeth, hygiene, diet, sleep).

- sticks up for me—speaks up if someone says something mean to or about me.

If the actual Parent Report Card is too intimidating, you can instead have a general discussion with the child: "If you were going to design a report card for parents, what would be on it?" This topic creates an interesting dialogue about how the child views the parental role and where the child sees a need for change in the parent/child relationship. It's also an opportunity to define and clarify what the parent's role is.

Family Change

 ## Challenge

The parents have separated or divorced.

 ## Goals

The child will have the resources and supports needed to manage the transition.

The child will have at least three coping strategies for coping during the transition.

 ## Skill: Coping with family change

Skills addressed include learning to view change as an opportunity, defining similarities and differences between households, and creating a plan for transition between homes.

 ## Interventions

KALEIDOSCOPES

Kaleidoscopes are an appropriate metaphor for change because kaleidoscope images constantly shift. It can be helpful to have a kaleidoscope for the child to play with and then have a discussion about how situations in the child's life are shifting and changing too.

Have the child explore the various images they can create using the kaleidoscope. Point out how each kaleidoscope image is the result of a unique mix of objects at the lens of the scope. Most kaleidoscopes use plastic or glass pieces, but there are others that use interesting materials such as springs, buttons, and charms. When you turn the kaleidoscope, the pieces move around and create different images.

Change, such as living in more than one home, is a lot like a kaleidoscope—the same "pieces" are there (e.g. love, shelter, food, clothing, rules and expectations, siblings, etc.), but it looks different in one house than the other. For example: bedtime might be early at one house, and late at the other; the pet at one house might be a hamster, and in the other home it's a cat; the child's older sister might act more protective and loving in one home, and then more defiant in the other.

It can be challenging for kids to understand and manage the changes that occur when their parents split up. Talking about it can be one way to support the child and to let the child know you are open to discussion about it.

AT THIS HOUSE, AT THAT HOUSE

At This House, At That House is a worksheet that helps the child define the expectations in each place where they reside or spend a lot of time. It is helpful for the child (and oftentimes the adults, too) to list the rules and expectations in each place so they can "see" how they overlap and differ between residences.

The worksheet can validate the challenges the child experiences from going back and forth between residences (e.g. there is a three-hour difference in bedtime between the two homes). The worksheet can also help the child to communicate these challenges to the adults in each home.

My To-and-From Plan

For children who live in more than one home, it is helpful to have a plan that facilitates the transition back and forth as smoothly as possible. Even in the best of circumstances, where the parents and/or providers communicate respectfully and agree on the rules and expectations, children can *still* experience transitional stress or fatigue going back and forth between homes. You may not be able to change the schedule or the situation, but you can add supports and strategies to help make the transition easier.

Help the child create a To-and-From Plan and write it in the boxes on the worksheet. The plan can include helpful suggestions such as: "When I get to Dad's house I need 15 minutes to settle in and put my things where they need to go" or "Pack my bag the night before" or "Make sure phone is charged and that I pack Mom's house key" or "Go to bed before 9 o'clock so I am not grumpy at Mom's house." Planning ahead creates smoother transitions.

AT THIS HOUSE, AT THAT HOUSE

*

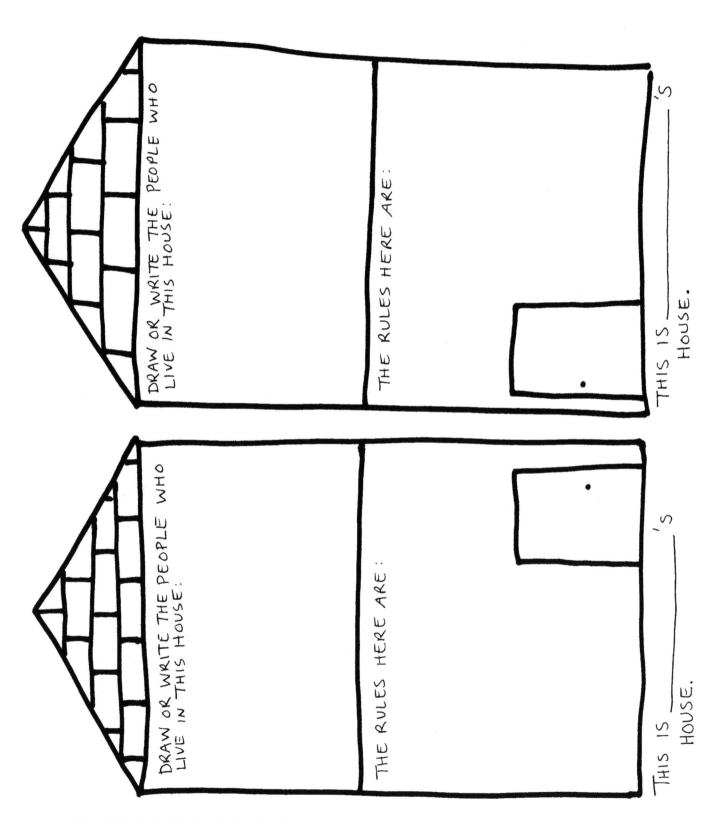

DRAW OR WRITE THE PEOPLE WHO LIVE IN THIS HOUSE:

THE RULES HERE ARE:

THIS IS _____'S HOUSE.

DRAW OR WRITE THE PEOPLE WHO LIVE IN THIS HOUSE:

THE RULES HERE ARE:

THIS IS _____'S HOUSE.

My "To-And-From" Plan

This is how I get ready to leave this house:

This is how I settle back in when I come back to this house:

If I start to feel unsettled or upset at this house I will do the following to help myself feel calmer or better:

This is _____'s house

This is _____'s house

Mental Illness and Addictions

 ## Challenge

The child loves someone who has a moderate to severe mental illness and/or substance abuse.

 ## Goals

The child will have a basic understanding of what mental illness and addiction are.

The child will have a safety plan, if necessary, in case the loved one is abusing substances and/or being unsafe (see worksheet).

 ## Skill: Learning about mental illness and addictions

Skills addressed include identifying the situation, providing education about the situation, planning for self-care, and creating a safety plan.

 ## Interventions

Mental illness and substance use/abuse are tough topics for families to address with younger family members. As a counselor I am often asked how and when it is appropriate to start sharing this information with the children who are affected by it (e.g. if the grandparents have guardianship of the child due to the parent's substance abuse and/or mental illness). Children are like antennae—they pick up on everything around them even if they can't process what they are seeing and hearing. The earlier you talk to your children about what is going on in their lives, the better. The key is to give simple, general information to children. The younger they are, the simpler the information needs to be. If the children are ready for more detailed information, they will ask for it. Here are some examples of ways to answer children's questions.

What is mental illness?

A GENERAL ANSWER FOR YOUNGER CHILDREN

Sometimes people's feelings, thoughts, or behaviors get stuck or even mixed up for a long period of time. We call that a mental illness. A mental illness can make a person act differently than we'd expect.

AN ANSWER FOR OLDER CHILDREN

An illness is something that makes you feel sick and/or yucky. When you have a *physical* illness, it means the illness makes your body, or part of your body, feel sick (e.g. when your throat hurts from a cold). When you have a *mental* illness, it means the illness makes your brain, your feelings, or even your behavior feel sick (e.g. when your heart feels sad, no matter how many amazing good things are happening for you).

Sometimes an illness is quick, like the flu. And some illnesses last a while. Mental illnesses typically last a while.

Mental illness comes in many different forms—one mental illness can look and feel different from another. Many mental illnesses affect a person's feelings. For example, imagine an emotion (e.g. sad, happy, worried, angry) and then pretend your brain gets stuck feeling *only* (or mostly) that emotion. Then imagine that your brain makes that emotion feel extra strong.

At first it might sound like fun to think of your brain getting stuck feeling super happy. But if you give this some thought, I bet you can think of ways in which this could cause trouble. For example, what if you were so happy that you couldn't sleep anymore? Or what if you found everything extremely fun or funny? Can you think of some times when this would actually be a bad thing?

Or think of the opposite—imagine if your brain got stuck feeling sad all the time, or worried all the time, or angry all the time. That sounds pretty exhausting, doesn't it?

Mental illnesses can also affect people's thoughts, like making a person think too many thoughts all at once for long periods of time. Some people with mental illness even see and hear things that are not real.

What are the names of mental illnesses?

Here are some mental illnesses you might have heard about:

- *Depression.* Someone who gets stuck feeling sad and lonely might have depression.

- *Mania.* Someone who gets stuck feeling intensely happy and/or agitated might have mania.

- *ADD/ADHD.* This means "attention deficit/hyperactivity disorder." People with ADD/ADHD might have a hard time sitting still or paying attention. Almost everybody has a hard time sitting still or paying attention sometimes, but people with ADHD feel this way almost every minute of the day.

- *Obsessive compulsive disorder (OCD).* This is a mental illness in which your brain becomes stuck thinking that it has to do the same thing over and over and over again. For one person that might mean, for example, feeling they have to tap the light switch 17 times before leaving a room. For another person it might mean they can't stop picking at their skin or pulling out their hair (e.g. their eyebrows). Others might have stuck thoughts where they can't stop thinking about something. As you can see, OCD can look and feel very different from one person to the next.

There are many types of mental illness—way too many to list here. But if you have more questions about mental illness talk to a trusted adult who can help you.

Can a person have more than one mental illness?

Yes! It's normal for people to have more than one mental illness. For example, a person might have attention deficit disorder (ADD), depression, and anxiety, which are all mental illnesses.

What if I get a mental illness? Does that mean I will have a bad life?

If you do get diagnosed with a mental illness at any point in your life, you should know that there are many ways to get the help and treatment to help you feel better. It's also good for you to know that you can have mental illness *and* have a beautiful, happy, full life.

Is there medicine people can take for mental illness?

Yes. There are many different medicines that treat mental illnesses. There are also many ways to treat the symptoms of mental illness without medicine.

What should I do if I think I might have a mental illness?

Talk to a trusted adult to let them know your concerns. Doctors, counselors, school guidance counselors, and social workers have specialized knowledge about the signs and symptoms of mental illness.

What should I do if I think someone I love has a mental illness?

Talk to a trusted adult, such as one of the professionals listed above, or talk to a family member you trust and feel safe with.

Someone I care about has a mental illness—what should I do?

Keep caring about them. And care for yourself too.

Mental illness can be hard on the people who experience it, and sometimes it's hard on the people who love them, too. If someone you love has a mental illness that causes some challenges or distress for you, make a plan for how to care for yourself when times get tough. There's a worksheet about it in this book to help you do so.

Are there times when mental illness is dangerous?

Yes. There are times when a mental illness can make someone want to hurt themselves or someone else. This can be confusing and scary for the person and their loved ones! It's important for those involved to have a safety plan. A safety plan is a plan that the family and/or loved ones agree to in case the loved one becomes unsafe for any reason.

If someone you love needs to stay at a hospital or crisis unit for a while, this may seem frightening. However, if this happens, remind yourself they will be safe there until they get the help they need to feel better and safer.

My Safety Plan

Fill out the sections below:

These are trusted people I can talk to about what is going on:

_____

_____

_____

_____

_____

These are things I can do to help me feel calmer, happier, and healthier in general:

_____

_____

_____

_____

_____

If things start to feel uncomfortable or unsafe where I live, I will do the following to stay safe:

_____

_____

_____

_____

_____

*

If I need a code word, I will create one and I will let the following people know about it:

_____

_____

_____

_____

_____

[A code word/phrase is used when you feel threatened, scared, or unsafe. It can be used with family or other emergency contacts that you trust. Make sure everyone knows the code word/phrase and there is a plan for what will happen when the word/phrase is used. For example, e.g. if you text the word "cornflake" to your aunt, she knows to come pick you up at the basketball court near your house right away.]

Emergency contacts—names, phone numbers, addresses:

_____

_____

_____

_____

_____

[Include family and friends of people who know what you are going through and who might be able to come pick you up or meet you somewhere. Also include any local emergency numbers such as 911, the police, child protection services, counselors, crisis numbers, and sponsors.]

What Is Addiction and Substance Abuse?

Sometimes older people drink alcohol because they enjoy it. Alcohol is safe for many people to drink in small amounts. But for some people alcohol can be dangerous because their bodies become addicted to it. Addicted means their bodies get tricked into needing the alcohol, rather than feeling like they can choose whether or not they want to drink it.

Like alcohol, people can get addicted to substances. "Substances" usually mean drugs. There are drugs of all kinds, many of which are okay and healthy for us to use, but the drugs I am talking about here are the ones that are *not* okay. They are the ones that are illegal. Some of these drugs are smoked, some are swallowed, and some are injected using needles.

When people get addicted to alcohol or drugs, it can make them act in ways that can be confusing, hurtful, and embarrassing.

Many children have a parent or loved one who is addicted to alcohol and/or drugs. This is a very tough situation for kids to deal with! If someone you love has an addiction, the most important thing for you to remember is that it is not your fault.

It's also important to talk to a safe and trusted adult, such as a family member, a counselor, or school guidance counsellor, who can offer support and help you find the resources you need. You can also fill out the safety plan in this book so you can refer to it if/when necessary.